THE ENCYCLOPEDIA OF
DESSERTS

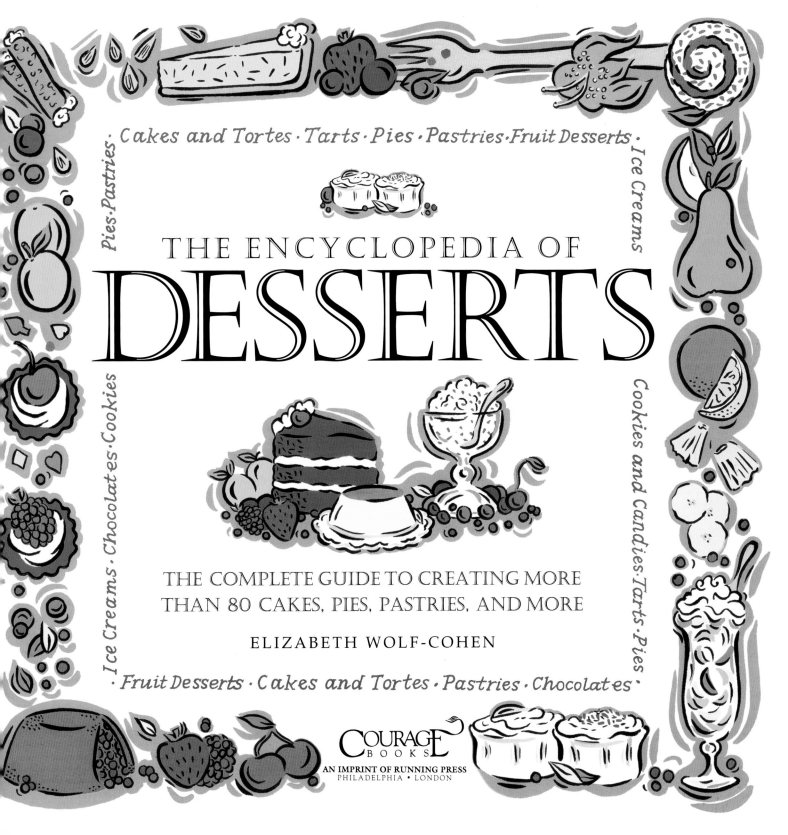

·Cakes and Tortes · Tarts · Pies · Pastries · Fruit Desserts ·

THE ENCYCLOPEDIA OF
DESSERTS

THE COMPLETE GUIDE TO CREATING MORE
THAN 80 CAKES, PIES, PASTRIES, AND MORE

ELIZABETH WOLF-COHEN

· Fruit Desserts · Cakes and Tortes · Pastries · Chocolates ·

COURAGE
BOOKS

AN IMPRINT OF RUNNING PRESS
PHILADELPHIA · LONDON

A QUINTET BOOK

© 1997 by Quintet Publishing Limited
Printed in Singapore by
Star Standard Industries (Pte) Ltd
9 8 7 6 5 4 3 2 1

Digit on the right indicates the number
of this printing

ISBN 0-7624-0105-2

Library of Congress
Cataloging-in-Publication Number 96-70067

This book was designed and produced by
Quintet Publishing Limited
6 Blundell Street
London N7 9BH

Creative Director: Richard Dewing
Art Director: Clare Reynolds
Designer: Ian Hunt
Project Editor: Kathy Steer
Editor: Anna Bennett
Illustrator: Joanne Makin

Typeset in Great Britain by
Central Southern Typesetters, Eastbourne
Manufactured in England by
D.P. Graphics, Holt, Wiltshire

Published by Courage Books an imprint of
Running Press Book Publishers
125 South Twenty-Second Street
Philadelphia, Pennsylvania 19103-4399

Contents

INTRODUCTION

I love desserts—I always have. As a child, desserts were only for special occasions and holidays. There was the occasional ginger bread cake or chocolate pudding, but on the whole after dinner there was fresh fruit. Maybe that explains my great passion for desserts.

Even now I get excited when I think of which dessert I should make when friends come around for dinner; somehow I always design the menu backwards—starting with the dessert and then deciding what the main course will be. When I eat out, I always read the dessert menu first to be sure I reserve something special, or order a soufflé or other dessert which has a twenty minute wait or just make sure I leave enough room for some extraordinarily rich confection. Dessert for me is a real pleasure. It makes a simple dinner or occasion into something special. I simply cannot resist them.

The Encyclopedia of Desserts is a compilation of desserts to die for—each one more tempting than the next. Some maybe as simple as the Bittersweet Chocolate Soufflés or the classic Créme Caramel, others maybe spectacular party pieces like the Celebration Brownie-baked Alaska, but they are all

heavenly. Each one is especially scrumptious in its way, even if simple in concept. A slice of Prune Coffee Cake with a foaming hot cappuccino on a wintry morning seems the ultimate pleasure at the time, while a bowl of cool, refreshing Tropical Fruit Salad with Thai-Scented Coconut Cream is just perfect on a hot, sultry night after a spicy barbecued meal.

Whatever the occasion, you'll find the perfect dessert in this collection. I have tried to include all the necessary techniques specific to different kinds of desserts, such as making perfect pastry, cooking custard without curdling and even successfully melting chocolate. Many recipes include tips for preparing ahead and ideas for decorating. Most of the equipment and ingredients required are found in the average kitchen or are available in cookware stores and supermarkets. Specialty items are explained and tips for finding them are given. Do make an effort to use the best quality ingredients you can afford, as the end result will be well worth it.

Whatever the occasion, or even if there is no occasion, a dessert shows family and friends you really care. Make one tonight and enjoy it.

CAKE MAKING

Cakes are among the world's favorite desserts. Many cakes have a long-standing tradition and often play a central role in celebrating special occasions from birthdays to weddings to christenings and many holidays as well. A perfect cake depends on good ingredients, the right utensils, careful measuring, and accurate temperatures and timing.

There are many methods of making cakes, but whatever preparation is used, make sure all ingredients are at room temperature unless otherwise instructed. Eggs should not be cold, as a temperature contrast can curdle a creamed butter-sugar mixture.

The type of pan will affect the baking time, as well as the finish of the cake. Dark metal pans reduce the cooking time slightly and encourage a darker crust; removeable-bottom pans help in unmolding of fragile or delicate cakes and tortes, springform pans are essential for cheesecakes and heavy-based high-sided pans prevent long cooking fruitcakes from scorching on the bottom. It is important to use the correct pan: always use the type specified in a recipe.

PREHEATING AND TESTING FOR DONENESS

Be sure to preheat your oven at least 15 minutes before baking and, if necessary, use an oven thermometer to verify the temperature. Most cakes should be baked on the center or bottom third shelf. If baking two or three layers, stagger the pans so they are not directly above each other and rotate them from front to back and top to bottom when the filling is adequately set.

There are several ways of testing for doneness. Using a cake tester is best for plain cakes which need to be baked through. Inserted into the center, it should come out clean with no crumbs attached. Alternatively, press a fingertip lightly onto the center of the cake: it should spring back if done. Most cakes should bake to a golden brown and tend to shrink slightly from the side of the pan.

Many cakes can be stored for two to three days, wrapped well in an airtight tin. For longer periods, refrigerate or freeze until needed.

PASTRY MAKING

Pastry is one of the great foundations of dessert making and by following a few basic rules everyone can make good pastry.

There are three basic pastries: pie crust – a short flaky pastry which can vary in thickness; *pâte feuilletée* or puff pastry, the basis of napoleons and other French pastries, and cream puff or *choux* pastry, used for cream puffs and profiteroles.

Pastry can be made by hand or in a food processor. If using a machine remember to not overwork the dough; always stop before it forms a ball or the pastry will be tough. "Resting the dough" is essential for all pastry as is chilling the dough. Chilling helps the resting process and sets the fat, allowing for easier handling and less shrinkage.

The ingredients for pastry should be weighed as this produces more accurate results, but you can also, as I have in this book, use the "scoop and sweep" method: Dip a solid 1-cup measure into a container of all-purpose flour and use a broad-bladed knife to level off any excess. If you wish, add 1/8 teaspoon of baking powder to each cup of flour to insure a light result. Alternatively, you can buy good-quality pastry from supermarkets.

LINING A TART PAN

The traditional tart pan is shallow with no rim. It has a fluted side and sometimes a removable bottom. This gives the characteristic edge and allows the side of the pan to be removed without disturbing the base. Flan rings are generally smooth-sided rings which are set on a heavy pastry sheet to form its bottom. The best pans are dull metal or nonstick, as shiny metal reflects the heat and prevents the crust from browning. Butter-rich dough does not generally stick, but I like to spray the pan lightly with a vegetable cooking spray. Alternatively, use a little oil.

1. To transfer rolled-out dough to a tart or pie pan, set the rolling pin on the near edge of the pastry round, square or rectangle. Fold the edge of the pastry over the rolling pin, then continue to roll dough loosely around pin.

2. Hold far edge of dough and rolling pin over far edge of the pan and gently unroll the dough, allowing it to settle into the pan without stretching or pulling. Using floured fingertips, lift outside edge of dough and ease into bottom and sides of pan, allowing excess pastry to overhang the edge.

3. To line a tart pan, smooth pastry onto the bottom of pan and press the overhang down slightly toward the center of the pan, making the top edge thicker. Roll the rolling pin over the edge, cutting off any excess dough and flattening the top edge. Press the thickened top edge against the side of the pan to form a stand-up edge. This makes the edge slightly thicker and higher, reinforcing the sides of the pastry case. Prick the bottom with a fork and, if you like, crimp or decorate the edge. Refrigerate 1 hour or freeze for 20 minutes.

LINING TARTLET PANS

For very small tartlet pans (less than 2 inches): Arrange the pans on the work surface close together and unroll the rolled-out pastry over them, loosely draping the dough into them. Roll the rolling pin over them to cut off the excess pastry then, using a floured thumb, press the pastry onto the bottom and up the sides of the pans. Prick bottoms with a fork. For larger tartlets, I prefer to follow the steps for lining a round tart pan, as this insures adequate pastry and a firm high edge to support any filling.

BLIND BAKING

Blind baking is a method of pre-baking a pastry case, either partially or completely, to prevent the pastry from becoming soggy and to ensure that the base cooks evenly and completely. Complete baking is necessary for an uncooked filling and partial blind baking is recommended when a liquid, creamy or custard-based filling is cooked completely in the pastry shell. The dough is generally weighted with dried beans, rice or pastry weights to prevent the pastry from shrinking and puffing too much.

1. Cut out a circle of baking parchment or foil about three inches larger than the tart pan. Fold in half and lay it across the center of the dough-lined tart pan. Unfold it and press onto the bottom, into the edge and up the sides of the dough.

2. Fill the lined tart shell with dried beans, rice or pastry weights and spread them evenly over the bottom and up the sides. The dried beans, rice or pastry weights can be cooled and saved to be reused.

3. To partially blind bake pastry: bake in a 400°F oven for 15–20 minutes until the pastry is set and rim looks dry and slightly golden. Carefully remove to a heatproof surface and remove the paper or foil and beans. The pastry shell can be filled and baking finished.

4. To completely blind bake pastry: Bake in a 400°F oven for 20 minutes. Remove to an heatproof surface and remove the paper or foil and beans. Prick the pastry bottom again with a fork and continue baking for 10 minutes or until golden. The bottom should look dry and set. Cool completely on a cooling rack before filling as recipe directs.

FRUIT DESSERTS

Fresh fruit forms the basis of many delicious desserts. In general, choose firm, yet ripe fruit for the best flavor. Fruit can be used fresh, cut-up, poached or puréed and in many other ways.

If using fresh fruit, sprinkle apples, pears, bananas, peaches, and nectarines with a little lemon juice to prevent them from darkening. A swivel-bladed vegetable peeler is the best choice for peeling and can be used to core apples and pears as well. Avoid washing delicate berries if possible, as they absorb water and lose their flavor. Scrub oranges, lemons, and limes if using the peel for zest or for julienne strips; better still, look for untreated and unwaxed fruits.

Poached fruits can be served on their own or used as a part of a more elaborate dessert. Always prepare the poaching syrup first, adding the flavorings as the recipe directs, and dissolving the sugar completely before adding the fruit. Adjust the heat so the syrup barely simmers, then cover the fruit with a piece of baking parchment or greaseproof paper. This helps to keep the fruit from floating and helps keep it immersed in the liquid. The cooking time will depend on the ripeness of the fruit; test by piercing the fruit with the blade of a sharp knife.

Puréed soft fruits make ideal sauces for desserts or can form the basis of other desserts. *Coulis* is a French word meaning a pourable purée and it is one of the easiest dessert sauces to make. Put a pound of fresh strawberries, raspberries, blackberries or mango or peach slices in a food processor fitted with a metal blade and process until smooth. Add sugar to taste and a little lemon juice, if you like, and process again. Press through a sieve and add a little liqueur, thinning with a little water if necessary.

FROZEN DESSERTS

Frozen desserts are an ideal choice for parties and occasions of all kinds, as the dessert can be made well ahead and even decorated, then stored in the freezer until you are almost ready to serve.

Homemade ice creams and sorbets can be served on their own or with a sauce or can be part of another dessert, like an ice cream pie or a Baked Alaska. If you enjoy making ice creams and frozen desserts, an electric ice-cream maker is a worthwhile investment.

If you don't have an ice-cream maker pour the mixture into a freezerproof container and freeze for 2 hours until it begins to freeze around the edges. Remove from the freezer and whisk until the mixture is blended. Continue for several hours until the mixture is frozen and smooth.

If adding any solids to the ice cream, such as chocolate chips, raisins, nuts or even a fruit or chocolate swirl, do so after the mixture has frozen, as these solid pieces will clog an ice-cream machine or a swirl will become too well blended. Be sure to freeze the ice cream mixture in a pretty bowl or glass dish if you plan to serve it at the table; otherwise a plastic freezer box with a tight-fitting lid will suffice.

To serve frozen desserts, allow to soften at room temperature for 15 minutes before serving, or 20–25 minutes in the refrigerator. For easier slicing, dip a thin-bladed knife into hot water before cutting (or an ice cream scoop for scooping) each slice; wipe off excess water.

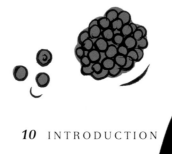

CUSTARDS, MOUSSES, AND SOUFFLES

Many popular desserts are based on a custard—a mixture of milk, eggs, and sugar, which is cooked over low heat until thickened or baked in the oven in a bain-marie to form a dessert on its own, like Crème Caramel or Crème Brûlée.

The most important factor in cooking custards is heat. If the custard mixture becomes too hot, or heats too quickly, the custard will curdle and separate. Cook custards over low heat in a heavy-based saucepan or use a double boiler or heatproof bowl set over hot water. Beat the egg yolks and sugar until foamy and lightened then pour the hot milk over the yolks, whisking constantly. This allows the milk to heat the egg mixture and start the cooking process. Return the mixture to the saucepan and stir constantly over low heat until the mixture thickens and coats the back of a spoon. If a custard does begin to curdle, remove from heat and whisk in an ice cube to lower the temperature, or strain into a cold bowl or saucepan.

Baked custards need to cook gently in a bain-marie or water bath, which insulates them from direct heat and helps prevent curdling. Setting the dessert on a folded dish towel provides more insulation for very delicate mixtures. To test a set custard, shake the pan; the center of the custard should wobble slightly, and a knife inserted halfway between the center and the edge should come out clean.

Mousses and soufflés generally use beaten egg whites to provide a light, airy texture. Often the egg yolks are beaten until thick and mousse-like to provide a base, then beaten egg whites are folded in. Put the egg whites in a large, grease-free bowl, preferably copper or stainless steel, and with an electric mixer or whisk, beat until foamy or "broken." If not using a copper bowl, add a pinch of cream of tartar or salt, which helps the whites to stiffen, and continue beating on a higher speed until the whites hold soft peaks when the beaters or whisk are lifted from the bowl.

For meringues, add about three quarters of the measured amount of sugar a tablespoon at a time, beating well after each addition until the sugar is dissolved (test by rubbing a little meringue between thumb and finger—if it feels gritty, continue beating). Continue beating until stiff and glossy. Sprinkle over the last quarter of the measured sugar all at once and gently fold in.

Folding is a method of combining a light mixture with a heavier one without deflating the lighter mixture. Do not overbeat the egg whites. Begin by stirring a spoonful of the beaten whites into the heavier mixture to lighten it, as this will allow the remaining whites to be incorporated more easily. Spoon over the remaining whites and fold in by cutting down into the center of the mixture to the bottom of the bowl, turning the mixture over itself with a rolling motion. Continue until the whites are just blended in but don't overwork the mixture or the whites will deflate.

If the whites are well beaten and stable, a mousse will have a firm yet light texture and will be able to support its own weight, and a soufflé will rise high in the oven to make a soft, light, and airy dessert.

Remember to butter the soufflé dish right up to the edge as it is the butter which helps lead the soufflé up the sides of the dish. To serve "crack" the top open with a spoon and serve each guest some of the firm top with some of the softer center—the ideal combination of textures.

CHAPTER ONE

Cakes
and
Tortes

Lime Coconut Layer Cake
with Seven-Minute Frosting

8–10 SERVINGS

Delicious layers of lime-scented sponge with a tangy lime custard topped with classic seven-minute frosting and coconut—a desert island dream dessert.

CAKE
1 cup all-purpose flour
Pinch of salt
6 eggs
3⁄4 cup sugar
Grated zest of 2 limes
1 tsp lime juice
3⁄4 cup shredded coconut

LIME CUSTARD
2 Tbsp cornstarch
1 cup cold water
2 eggs
Grated zest and juice of 1 large lime
1 cup sugar
6 Tbsp butter

SEVEN-MINUTE FROSTING
2 egg whites
11⁄2 cups sugar
3 Tbsp cold water
1⁄4 tsp cream of tartar
11⁄2 tsp light corn syrup
11⁄2 Tbsp lime juice
1 cup shredded coconut

1. Preheat oven to 350°F. Lightly grease three 8-inch cake pans. Line the bottom of each with nonstick baking parchment; regrease and flour pans. Sift the flour and salt.

2. Put the eggs in a large heatproof bowl and set over a saucepan of just simmering water. With an electric mixer, beat until frothy. Gradually beat in the sugar until well-blended. Continue beating until the mixture is doubled in volume and very thick.

3. Remove the bowl from the pan of water and fold in the grated lime zest, juice, and shredded coconut. Sift the flour mixture in three batches, folding in after each addition.

4. Divide the mixture evenly among the pans. Bake about 30 minutes. Cool for 5 minutes. Unmold onto a wire rack to cool completely.

5. Prepare the lime custard: Blend the cornstarch with about a tablespoon of the cold water to dissolve. Whisk in the remaining eggs. Put the remaining water, grated zest and lime juice, sugar, and butter in a saucepan and, over medium heat, bring to a boil. Whisk a little of the mixture into the beaten egg mixture, then whisk the egg mixture into the saucepan and return to the heat. Whisk until the mixture boils, about 5 minutes. Pour into a bowl and cool.

6. Prepare the frosting: Put all the ingredients except the coconut in a heatproof mixing bowl and set over a saucepan of just simmering water. With an electric mixer, beat for 7 minutes until thick. Remove from the hot water and beat until mixture is at room temperature. Cover with plastic wrap.

7. Remove the paper from the cake layers. Place a layer on a plate and spread with half the lime custard. Cover with a second layer and the remaining lime custard. Spread the top and side of the cake with the frosting and press some of the shredded coconut onto the side of the cake; sprinkle the remaining coconut over the top.

White Chocolate Mousse and Strawberry Layer Cake

10 SERVINGS

Other fresh berries in season can be used in this cake, but strawberries look particularly elegant.

4 oz good-quality white chocolate, grated or chopped
1⁄2 cup heavy cream
1⁄2 cup milk
1 Tbsp rum or vanilla extract
2 cups all-purpose flour
1 tsp baking powder
Pinch of salt
1⁄2 cup (1 stick) unsalted butter, softened
3⁄4 cup sugar
3 eggs
11⁄2 lb fresh strawberries, sliced, plus extra for decoration
3 cups heavy cream
2 Tbsp rum or strawberry-flavored liqueur
1 Tbsp confectioners' sugar, sifted

WHITE CHOCOLATE MOUSSE FILLING

10 oz good-quality white chocolate, chopped
11⁄2 cups heavy cream
2 Tbsp rum or strawberry-flavored liqueur

1. Preheat oven to 350°F. Lightly butter two deep 9-inch cake pans. Line bottoms with nonstick baking parchment; regrease and flour pans. Put the white chocolate and cream in a saucepan and stir over low heat until melted and smooth. Stir in the milk and rum or vanilla extract. Cool.

2. Sift together the flour, baking powder, and salt. Set aside. With an electric mixer, beat the butter and sugar until light and creamy. Add the eggs, one at a time, beating well after each addition.

3. Add the flour mixture alternately with the melted chocolate mixture in three batches until just blended. Scrape into the prepared pans and bake 20–25 minutes or until done. Cool in pans 10 minutes. Unmold onto a wire rack to cool completely.

4. Prepare the mousse. Process the chopped white chocolate in a food processor 15–30 seconds. Bring the cream to a boil. Pour the hot cream through the processor feed tube and process until smooth. Pour into a bowl, stir in the rum or strawberry-flavored liqueur and refrigerate until just set. Whisk until light and mousse-like.

5. To assemble: Remove the paper from cake bottoms. Slice each cake into two layers. Place one layer, cut-side up, on a cake plate and spread with one third of the mousse mixture. Arrange one third of the sliced strawberries over the mousse. Place a second layer on top and continue layering in this way. Cover with the last cake layer.

6. Whip the cream with the rum or liqueur and confectioners' sugar until firm peaks form. Spread half over top and sides of cake. Pipe scrolls or rosettes with remaining cream around top edge of cake and in the center. Decorate with remaining strawberries.

Jewish Apple Cake

10–12 SERVINGS

Apple cakes are traditionally popular in the Jewish community. This one is made with oil, keeping it moist and giving it a rich texture.

APPLE FILLING
2 lb cooking apples, peeled, cored and thinly sliced
4 Tbsp sugar
1 tsp ground cinnamon
Grated zest and juice of 1 lemon

CAKE
4 eggs
1¼ cups superfine sugar
1 cup plus 2 Tbsp vegetable oil
1⅔ cups all-purpose flour
2 tsp baking powder
1½ tsp vanilla extract
3 to 4 Tbsp granulated sugar for sprinkling

1. Preheat oven to 350°F. Grease and lightly flour a 9 x 13-inch cake pan, preferably nonstick. Toss the apple slices with sugar, cinnamon, lemon zest, and juice.

2. With an electric mixer, beat the eggs with the sugar until thick and pale and the mixture leaves a ribbon trail, 7 minutes. Gradually beat in the oil until blended. Fold in flour, baking powder, and vanilla.

3. Pour half the batter into the pan, spreading evenly. Spoon half the apple mixture over the batter. Cover the apple mixture with the remaining batter and top with the remaining apple mixture, spreading it into an even layer. Sprinkle generously with sugar.

4. Bake until cake is golden and puffed and apples are tender and the center springs back when pressed gently with a fingertip, 1¼–1½ hours. Cover with foil if the top browns too quickly. Remove to a wire rack and cool 30 minutes in the tin. Serve warm or at room temperature.

Devil's Food Dream Cake

10–12 SERVINGS

These rich, dark chocolate layers are filled and frosted with a dark chocolate ganache, a chocolate truffle filling. Truly the work of a devil's dream.

1/4 cup unsweetened cocoa powder
2 1/4 cups cake flour
2 tsp baking soda
1/2 tsp salt
2 squares (2 oz) unsweetened chocolate, chopped
1/2 cup (1 stick) unsalted butter, softened
2 1/2 cups light brown sugar, lightly packed
2 tsp vanilla extract
3 eggs
3/4 cup sour cream or buttermilk
1 tsp vinegar
1 cup boiling water

CHOCOLATE GANACHE FROSTING
3 cups heavy cream
1 1/2 lb good-quality bittersweet or semisweet chocolate, chopped
2 Tbsp butter
1 Tbsp vanilla extract

1. Preheat oven to 375°F. Grease two 9-inch cake pans. Line bottoms with nonstick baking parchment; regrease and flour pans. Sift together the cocoa powder, cake flour, baking soda, and salt; set aside.

2. In the top of a double-boiler over low heat, melt the chocolate, stirring frequently until smooth. Cool.

3. With an electric mixer, beat the butter, brown sugar, and vanilla until light and creamy. Add the eggs, one at a time, beating well after each addition.

4. Add the flour mixture alternately with the sour cream or buttermilk in three batches. Stir in the vinegar and slowly beat in the boiling water. Pour into the pans and bake 20–25 minutes. Cool cakes in their pans 5 minutes. Carefully unmold onto a wire rack to cool completely.

5. Prepare the frosting: Bring the cream to a boil. Remove from heat and add the chocolate all at once, stirring until melted. Beat in the butter and vanilla. Pour into a bowl and refrigerate until the ganache reaches a spreading consistency.

6. To assemble: Remove paper from cake bottoms. Slice each cake into two layers. Place one layer, cut side up on a plate and spread with one sixth of ganache. Place second layer on top and frost with another sixth of ganache. Continue layering. Frost the top and sides of cake with remaining ganache.

Chocolate Pecan Torte

12–16 SERVINGS

A torte is a European-style cake which generally uses ground nuts or bread crumbs instead of flour to bind the eggs and butter. This torte is extremely rich and a little goes a long way.

1 1/4 cups pecan pieces
1/2 cup superfine sugar
7 oz good-quality bittersweet or semisweet chocolate, chopped
10 Tbsp unsalted butter, cut into pieces
4 eggs
1 tsp rum or vanilla extract
1 tsp ground cinnamon
24 toasted pecan halves for decoration (optional)

CHOCOLATE-HONEY GLAZE
4 oz bittersweet or semisweet chocolate, chopped
4 Tbsp unsalted butter, cut into pieces
2 Tbsp honey
1/2 tsp ground cinnamon

1. Preheat oven to 350°F. Spread the pecans on a cookie sheet and toast until lightly browned, 3–5 minutes. When cool, process in a food processor with 1 tablespoon of the sugar for 30–45 seconds until fine crumbs form. (Do not overprocess.)

2. Butter an 8-inch cake pan, line the bottom with nonstick baking parchment and butter again. Melt the chocolate and butter until smooth, remove from heat, and cool slightly.

3. Beat the eggs with the remaining sugar and rum or vanilla extract until frothy. Beat in the melted chocolate, then stir in the ground pecans and cinnamon. Pour into the pan.

4. Place the cake pan into a roasting pan and pour in enough boiling water to come 3/4 inch up the side of the cake pan. Bake 25–30 minutes until the edge of the torte is set, but the center is slightly soft. Remove to a wire rack to cool.

5. Prepare the glaze: Heat the chocolate, butter, honey, and cinnamon until melted, stirring constantly; remove from heat. Dip each pecan half halfway into the glaze, allow excess to drain off and place on a nonstick baking parchment-lined cookie sheet until set.

6. Loosen the torte from the side of the pan with a knife. Unmold onto a wire rack placed over a cookie sheet. Remove the lining paper. Pour the glaze over the top of the torte and spread evenly. Allow to set slightly, then arrange the chocolate-dipped nuts around the outside edge of the torte and allow the glaze to set completely. Refrigerate at least 2 hours or overnight. Serve at room temperature.

Rich Lemon Pound Cake

8–10 SERVINGS

1 2/3 cups all-purpose flour
2 tsp baking powder
1/4 tsp salt
1 cup (2 sticks) unsalted butter, softened
1 cup superfine sugar
4 eggs, lightly beaten
Grated zest of 1 lemon
1 tsp lemon extract
1/2 tsp vanilla extract

LEMON GLAZE
1 cup confectioners' sugar, sifted
2 to 4 Tbsp lemon juice

1. Preheat oven to 325°F. Grease and flour an 8 x 4-inch loaf pan. Sift together the flour, baking powder, and salt.

2. With an electric mixer, beat the butter at medium speed until soft. Gradually add the sugar and then beat until light and creamy, 5 minutes.

3. Add the beaten eggs a tablespoon at a time, beating well after each addition. If the mixture begins to curdle, sprinkle in a little of the flour mixture.

4. Add the flour mixture in three batches, folding in lightly with a spoon until just blended. Stir in the lemon zest, lemon extract, and vanilla extract.

5. Scrape the batter gently into the pan, smoothing the top and making a slight indentation along the center. Bake 30 minutes until golden and the center springs back when pressed with a fingertip.

6. Remove to a wire rack and cool in the pan 10 minutes. Unmold onto the wire rack and turn top-side up to cool completely.

7. Sift the confectioners' sugar into a small bowl and gradually stir in enough lemon juice until a smooth glaze is formed. Gently spoon over the warm cake and allow to set before slicing.

Prune Coffee Cake

10–12 SERVINGS

My Polish neighbors serve this cake with mid-morning coffee. The chocolate glaze makes this cake extra special.

3 cups all-purpose flour
1½ tsp baking soda
1 tsp baking powder
1 cup (2 sticks) unsalted butter, cut into pieces
Grated zest of 1 orange
2 cups sugar
1 Tbsp vanilla or rum extract
¼ tsp salt
2 cups sour cream
3 eggs, lightly beaten
¾ cup prune purée*
½ cup chopped walnuts or pecans
2 Tbsp unsweetened cocoa powder, sifted
1 tsp ground cinnamon

CHOCOLATE-HONEY GLAZE
3 oz bittersweet or semisweet chocolate, chopped
3 Tbsp unsalted butter
1½ Tbsp honey

1. Preheat oven to 350°F. Grease and flour a heavy 10-inch Bundt pan (preferably nonstick). Sift the flour, baking soda, and baking powder.

2. Melt the butter in a saucepan. Stir in the orange zest and remove from heat. Immediately stir in the sugar, vanilla or rum extract, salt, sour cream, and eggs, then beat in all the flour mixture until blended.

3. Spoon about half the batter into the pan. Stir the prune purée and drop heaped tablespoonsfuls over the center of the batter. Sprinkle the walnuts or pecans, cocoa powder, and ground cinnamon over the top of the prune purée.

4. Spoon the remaining batter over the prune purée and nut mixture and smooth the top evenly. Draw a palette knife through the mixtures creating a swirling pattern. Bake 50 minutes. Cool in the pan 10 minutes.

5. Invert the cake onto a wire rack to cool completely. Melt the chocolate, butter, and honey. Drizzle the glaze over the cake and allow to set.

*Prune purée, sometimes called *lekvar,* is used in Eastern European and Jewish baking. It can be found in large supermarkets or delicatessens or specialty stores. To make your own, simmer 1 cup dried prunes with 1⁄2 cup water, a little grated orange zest and about 2 tablespoons orange juice until all the liquid is absorbed and the prunes form a mushy purée. Blend in a food processor. Store, covered, in the refrigerator.

Blueberry Cream Cheese Streusel Cake

10–12 SERVINGS

This delicious cake is a cross between a blueberry muffin and a cheese Danish—perfect with cappuccino.

STREUSEL TOPPING
1⁄2 cup (1 stick) unsalted butter, softened
2⁄3 cup sugar
1⁄3 cup light brown sugar, lightly packed
2⁄3 cup all-purpose flour
1⁄2 cup chopped toasted almonds
11⁄2 tsp ground cinnamon
1⁄2 tsp freshly ground nutmeg
1⁄4 tsp salt

CREAM CHEESE FILLING
12 oz cream cheese
1⁄3 cup sugar
1 egg
1 Tbsp lemon juice
1 tsp almond extract

CAKE
4 cups all-purpose flour
4 tsp baking powder
1 tsp salt
1⁄2 cup (1 stick) unsalted butter, softened
11⁄4 cups sugar
2 eggs
1 tsp almond extract
1 cup milk
3 cups fresh blueberries

1. Preheat oven to 375°F. Generously butter a 13 x 9-inch ovenproof glass baking dish (do not use metal or porcelain). Prepare the streusel: With a pastry blender or fingertips, rub together all the ingredients until large crumbs form.

2. Prepare the filling: With an electric mixer, beat the cream cheese and sugar until creamy. Beat in the egg, lemon juice, and almond extract.

3. Prepare the cake: Sift together the flour, baking powder, and salt. With an electric mixer, beat the butter and sugar until creamy, about 3 minutes. Beat in the eggs, one at a time, beating well after each addition. Beat in the almond extract. On low speed, beat in the flour mixture alternately with the milk, and ending with the flour mixture. Carefully fold in all the blueberries.

4. Spread slightly less than half the cake mixture over the bottom of the dish. Spread the filling over the batter. Sprinkle over one quarter of the streusel topping. Drop spoonfuls of remaining batter over the top and spread evenly. Sprinkle on remaining topping. Bake 1 hour until crunchy and golden brown.

5. Remove to a wire rack and cool completely in the dish. Cut into squares and serve.

Chocolate-Almond Zuccotto

12–14 SERVINGS

Chocolate Roulade Cake (p. 24)
2 Tbsp almond-flavored liqueur

CHOCOLATE-ALMOND FILLING
2 cups heavy cream
1 lb ricotta cheese
1/2 cup sugar
4 Tbsp almond-flavored liqueur
6 oz semisweet chocolate, melted
3 oz semisweet chocolate, grated
1/2 cup chopped almonds, lightly toasted

CHOCOLATE WHIPPED CREAM
10 oz good-quality bittersweet or semisweet chocolate, chopped
2 cups heavy cream
2 Tbsp almond-flavored liqueur
1/2 cup chopped almonds, lightly toasted

1. Cool roulade. Cut out an 8-inch circle from cake. Cut remaining long strip of cake into long narrow triangles, 2 inches at base end, and cut any remaining cake into pieces. Sprinkle with liqueur.

2. Line bowl with plastic wrap, then with the point of each triangle in the center of the bowl, line with the triangles; using any cake pieces to fill in gaps.

3. Beat the cream until stiff peaks form. Beat the ricotta with the sugar, and liqueur. Stir a spoonful of cream into the ricotta, fold in remaining cream. Remove half the mixture to the "cream" bowl.

4. Fold the melted chocolate into one half of the ricotta-cream mixture. Fold the grated chocolate and almonds into the other half. Spoon the chocolate-almond mixture into the cake-lined bowl and spread on the base and up the sides, covering the cake and smoothing the edge. Spoon the melted chocolate-

ricotta mixture into the center. Cover with the 8-inch cake rounds, pressing down to compact the dessert. Refrigerate overnight.

5. Prepare the chocolate cream: Heat the chocolate in a heatproof bowl set over a saucepan of simmering water. Stir until melted and smooth. Cool. Beat the cream with the liqueur until soft peaks form. Fold the chocolate into the cream.

6. Unmold onto a plate. Peel off plastic wrap and spread the chocolate cream over the top and sides. Sprinkle over the almonds and refrigerate.

Carrot Cake with Maple Cream Cheese "Frosting"

10–12 SERVINGS

11/2 cups all-purpose flour
2 tsp baking powder
1/2 tsp baking soda
1/2 tsp salt
2 tsp ground cinnamon
1 tsp ground allspice
1 tsp ground ginger
1 Tbsp grated orange zest
4 eggs
1 cup dark brown sugar, firmly packed
1/2 cup sugar
11/4 cups vegetable oil
1 Tbsp vanilla extract
1 lb sweet carrots, grated
1 cup chopped walnuts or pecans
1/2 cup raisins
1/2 cup golden raisins

MAPLE CREAM CHEESE FROSTING
2 x 8 oz packages cream cheese, softened
21/2 cups confectioners' sugar, sifted
1/3 cup maple syrup
2 to 4 Tbsp milk to dilute if necessary
11/2 cups finely chopped toasted walnuts for decoration (optional)

1. Preheat oven to 350°F. Grease two 9-inch cake pans. Line the bottoms with baking parchment; and regrease. Dust lightly with flour. Sift together the flour, baking powder, baking soda, salt, cinnamon, allspice, and ginger. Stir in the orange zest.

2. Beat eggs until blended. Add sugars and beat well. Slowly beat in the oil, then the vanilla extract. Stir in the flour mixture in three batches then stir in the carrots, walnuts or pecans, raisins, and golden raisins. Divide the batter between the pans. Bake 25 minutes. Cool in pan 10 minutes, then unmold onto a wire rack and cool completely. Remove paper.

3. Prepare the frosting: With an electric mixer, beat the cream cheese. Gradually beat in the sugar until fluffy. Beat in maple syrup until spreadable. If necessary add a little milk to thin.

4. Put one cake layer on a plate, bottom-side down and spread with one quarter of frosting. Cover with second cake layer, rounded-side up. Spread top and side of cake with remaining frosting. Decorate with finely chopped walnuts if desired. Refrigerate 1 hour to set the frosting.

Chocolate Decadence

10–12 SERVINGS

CHOCOLATE MOUSSE CAKE
10 oz good-quality bittersweet chocolate, chopped
1/2 cup (1 stick) unsalted butter
8 eggs, separated
1/4 cup raspberry-flavored liqueur
1/4 tsp cream of tartar

CHOCOLATE RASPBERRY GANACHE FILLING
12 oz good-quality bittersweet chocolate, chopped
6 oz (11/2 sticks) unsalted butter, cut into pieces
1/2 cup seedless raspberry preserves
1/4 cup raspberry-flavored liqueur

CHOCOLATE-RASPBERRY GLAZE
1 cup heavy cream
8 oz good-quality bittersweet chocolate, chopped
2 Tbsp raspberry-flavored liqueur
1/2 cup fresh raspberries for decoration
Confectioners' sugar for dusting, sifted

1. Preheat oven to 350°F. Lightly butter two 9-inch springform pans. Line the bottoms with nonstick baking parchment and butter again.

2. Heat the chocolate and butter. Beat the egg yolks then gradually whisk into the melted chocolate. Whisk in the raspberry-flavored liqueur.

3. Beat the egg whites until frothy. Add the cream of tartar and continue beating until soft peaks form. Fold the whites into the chocolate-egg mixture.

4. Divide the mixture evenly between the two pans. Bake 35 minutes. Remove cakes to a wire rack to cool for 15 minutes. Remove sides of the pans and cool cakes. Invert onto a rack, remove pan bottoms and peel off paper.

5. Heat the chocolate, butter, and half the raspberry preserves for the filling. Remove from heat and stir in half the raspberry-flavored liqueur. Heat the remaining preserves and liqueur. Spread a thin layer of the preserve mixture over each cake layer.

6. Place one cake layer in cleaned pan, preserve side up. Spread with filling. Top with second cake layer, preserve-side down against filling. Refrigerate overnight.

7. Prepare the glaze. Bring the cream to a boil. Remove from heat and add in the chocolate all at once stirring until melted and smooth. Stir in the raspberry-flavored liqueur and set aside to cool. Remove the side of the springform pan. Transfer the cake to a wire rack set over a baking sheet. Pour the glaze over the cake, smooth the top and sides and allow to set. Scrape remaining glaze off the baking sheet back into the bowl and whisk until smooth. Pipe a scroll border around the edge of cake. Decorate with raspberries and dust with confectioners' sugar.

Cranberry-Orange Upside-Down Cake
with Orange Sauce

8 SERVINGS

"Upside-down" cakes became very popular in America in the 1940s, the most famous being made with canned pineapple rings.

ORANGE SAUCE
1 Tbsp cornstarch
1 cup freshly squeezed orange juice, strained
Grated zest of 1 orange
1/4 cup sugar
2 Tbsp unsalted butter

CRANBERRY TOPPING
4 Tbsp unsalted butter, melted
2 cups fresh cranberries
2/3 cup sugar
Grated zest of 1 orange
1/4 tsp ground cinnamon

CAKE
2/3 cup all-purpose flour
1 tsp baking powder
1/4 tsp salt
3 eggs
1/2 cup sugar
1/2 tsp vanilla extract
Grated zest of 1 orange
3 Tbsp unsalted butter, melted

1. Prepare the orange sauce: Put the cornstarch into a saucepan and whisk in the orange juice until the cornstarch is dissolved. Whisk in the orange zest, sugar and add the butter, then bring to a boil, whisking constantly for 1 minute until thickened. Simmer about 2 minutes. Remove from heat and cool.

2. Preheat oven to 350°F. Pour the melted butter into a 9-inch cake pan. Mix the cranberries, sugar, orange zest, and sugar in a bowl. Spread the mixture over the bottom of the pan, pressing gently into the butter.

3. Sift the flour, baking powder, and salt twice. Put the eggs in a heatproof bowl and set over a pan of simmering water. With an electric mixer, beat until frothy. Gradually beat in the sugar until thick and pale. Beat in the vanilla extract and orange zest.

4. Remove from heat and fold in the flour mixture in three batches; drizzle in the melted butter and fold into the batter. Spoon batter over the cranberry layer. Bake 35 minutes. Remove to a wire rack to cool, about 7 minutes.

5. Run a knife around the edge of the pan to loosen the cake. Place a plate over the pan, bottom side up, and quickly unmold the cake. Serve with the sauce.

Rose Petal Jam Cake
with Wild Strawberries

8 SERVINGS

1 cup all-purpose flour
1 tsp baking powder
Pinch of salt
5 Tbsp unsalted butter, softened
1/2 cup superfine sugar
1 large egg, lightly beaten
3 Tbsp rosewater*
1/4 cup milk
1/2 cup rose petal jam*

ROSE-SCENTED WHIPPED CREAM
1 cup heavy cream
1 Tbsp rosewater
1 Tbsp confectioners' sugar, sifted
1 cup wild strawberries

1. Preheat oven to 350°F. Grease and flour a 9-inch cake pan. In a large bowl sift together the flour, baking powder, and salt.

2. With an electric mixer, beat the butter and sugar until light and creamy, 5 minutes. Gradually beat in the egg and a tablespoon of rosewater. On low speed, beat in the flour mixture and the milk alternately in three batches ending with the flour mixture.

3. Scrape the batter into the prepared pan. Bake about 25 minutes or until done. Remove to a wire rack and cool in the pan 5 minutes. Turn out cake top-side up onto the wire rack to cool completely.

4. Split cake into two layers. Drizzle a tablespoon of rosewater over each cut surface. Allow to soak in for a few minutes. Lightly beat the jam and spread onto the cut-side of the bottom half of the cake.

5. With an electric mixer beat the cream with the rosewater and confectioners' sugar. Spread about half the whipped cream over the jam and sprinkle with half the wild strawberries. Top with the second cake layer rounded-side up and spread the remaining cream over the top swirling decoratively; sprinkle over remaining strawberries and dust with a little more confectioners' sugar. This cake is best eaten the day it is made.

*Rosewater and rose petal jam can be found in some large supermarkets, specialty stores, and Middle Eastern grocery stores.

Christmas Fruitcake

16 SERVINGS

This is a delicious, moist fruitcake; that keeps well it is ideal for the holiday season. After tasting this cake at a friend's house, I begged for the recipe from her Auntie Margaret who sent it from Monaghan, Ireland.

1²⁄3 cups self-rising flour
1 tsp baking soda
1 tsp ground cinnamon
1 tsp mixed spice
1 tsp ground ginger
1⁄4 tsp salt
1⁄2 cup (1 stick) butter
1⁄2 cup soft light brown sugar, lightly packed
1 (13¹⁄2-oz) can crushed pineapple
1 cup raisins, not packed down
1 cup golden raisins, not packed down
1 cup currants, not packed down
1 cup crystallized ginger, finely chopped
1⁄2 cup glacé cherries, chopped
1⁄2 cup mixed candied peel
2 eggs, lightly beaten
Pecan halves for decoration (optional)
Glacé cherries, halved, for decoration (optional)
2 to 3 Tbsp honey or marmalade for glazing

1. Sift the flour, baking soda, ground cinnamon, mixed spice, ground ginger, and salt into a bowl and set aside. Melt the butter and sugar in a saucepan until the sugar has dissolved, stirring frequently.

2. Add the pineapple with its juices and stir in dried fruits and ginger. Bring to a boil and simmer 3 minutes, stirring. Remove from heat and cool.

3. Preheat oven to 325°F. Grease an 8 x 3-inch nonstick cake pan with removeable bottom. Line the bottom and sides with baking parchment; regrease and lightly flour.

4. When cool, add the fruit mixture to the flour mixture with the glacé cherries and mixed peel. Stir in the beaten eggs and spoon into the pan and smooth the top. Arrange circles of pecan and cherry halves on the top pressing gently into the batter.

5. Bake 1 hour 20 minutes or until a skewer inserted into the center comes out clean. If cake colors too quickly, lower the temperature slightly and cover the top with a piece of foil. Remove to a wire rack to cool 30 minutes before unmolding. Turn cake right-side up and cool completely. Melt the honey or marmalade and brush over the top.

Chocolate Roulade
with White Chocolate Cream and Black Cherry Compote

12–14 SERVINGS

This cake is based on the classic Black Forest Cake—a combination of a rich dark chocolate roulade filled with a luscious white chocolate cream and served with a fresh cherry compote.

BLACK CHERRY COMPOTE
$2 \over 3$ cup water
6 Tbsp sugar
2 Tbsp fresh lemon or orange juice
1 vanilla bean, halved lengthwise or
1 Tbsp vanilla extract
1 lb (about 2$1 \over 2$ cups) fresh black cherries, pitted, and
halved if you like

CHOCOLATE GANACHE FROSTING
1$1 \over 4$ cups heavy cream
12 oz bittersweet or semisweet chocolate, chopped
2 Tbsp Kirsch or cognac

CAKE
5 eggs, separated
3 Tbsp unsweetened cocoa powder, plus extra for
dusting, sifted
Pinch of cream of tartar
1 cup confectioners' sugar, plus extra for dusting,
sifted

WHITE CHOCOLATE CREAM FILLING
7 oz good-quality white chocolate, chopped
2 cups heavy cream
2 Tbsp Kirsch

1. Prepare the compote: In a saucepan combine the water, sugar, lemon, or orange juice and vanilla bean or extract. Bring to a boil, stirring until the sugar has dissolved. Boil 3–4 minutes until thickened, then stir in the cherries. Simmer 1 minute. Cool. Remove the vanilla bean and pour compote into a bowl. Cover and refrigerate.

2. Prepare the frosting: Bring the cream to a boil. Remove from heat and add the chocolate all at once, stirring until melted. Strain into a bowl, stir in the Kirsch or cognac, and cool. Refrigerate at least 2 hours or until set.

3. Prepare the cake: Preheat oven to 400°F. Grease a 15$1 \over 2$ x 10$1 \over 2$-inch jelly-roll pan and line with nonstick baking parchment. With an electric mixer, beat the egg yolks until thick and creamy, about 5 minutes. Beat in the cocoa and half the confectioners' sugar. Set aside.

4. Beat the egg whites until frothy. Add the cream of tartar and beat until soft peaks form. Add the remaining confectioners' sugar 2 tablespoons at a time, beating well until stiff and glossy. Stir a spoonful of the whites into the yolk mixture, then gently fold the yolk mixture into the whites and spread the batter into the pan. Bake about 15 minutes.

5. Lay a clean dish towel on a work surface and cover with nonstick baking parchment, dust with cocoa or confectioners' sugar. Turn cake onto paper and peel off the lining paper. Starting from one narrow end, roll cake with the paper and towel, jelly-roll fashion. Cool on a wire rack.

6. Prepare the filling: Over low heat, heat the white chocolate with $1 \over 2$ cup of the cream until melted. Strain and cool. With an electric mixer, beat the remaining cream with the Kirsch until soft peaks form. Stir a spoonful of the cream into the white chocolate mixture then fold it into the remaining cream.

7. To assemble: Unroll the cooled cake and spread with the white chocolate cream. Reroll the cake without the paper. Transfer to a serving plate. Beat frosting until slightly lightened in color and texture, about 30 seconds; do not overbeat. Spread over roulade. Dust with confectioners' sugar and serve with the compote.

CHAPTER TWO

PIES, PASTRIES, and TARTS

Basic Sweet Pie Crust

1 cup all-purpose flour
1/2 tsp salt
3 to 4 Tbsp confectioners' sugar, sifted
1/2 cup cold unsalted butter (8 Tbsp), cut into
small pieces
2 egg yolks
2 Tbsp ice water
1/2 tsp vanilla extract (optional)

VARIATION "EXTRA SWEET TART CRUST"
1 cup all-purpose flour
1/2 tsp salt
4 to 5 Tbsp confectioners' sugar, sifted
1/2 cup cold unsalted butter (8 Tbsp),
cut into small pieces
3 egg yolks
1 Tbsp ice water
1/2 tsp vanilla extract (optional)

1. Process the flour, salt, and sugar in a food processor for 5 seconds. Sprinkle the butter over the flour mixture and process about 15 seconds until the mixture resembles coarse crumbs.

2. Beat the egg yolks with the ice water and vanilla and with the machine running, pour through the feed tube. Process just until the dough begins to hold together. DO NOT OVERPROCESS. Test by pinching a piece of dough between your fingers. If it is still crumbly add a little more water and pulse once or twice. Do not allow dough to form into a ball or the pastry will be tough. Turn out onto a sheet of plastic wrap.

3. Using the plastic wrap as a guide, hold each side with one hand and gently push the dough away from you, turning the dough and holding the opposite sides of the plastic wrap to contain the dough, until the dough is smooth and just blended. Flatten into a disk shape and wrap with the plastic wrap. Refrigerate 1 hour or overnight. Allow pastry to soften slightly at room temperature before using.

Crumb Crust

Ideal for chilled tarts. Particularly good for ice cream tarts and chilled mixtures. Use vanilla, chocolate, amaretti cookies (about 24) or gingersnaps (24–26) instead of Graham crackers or replace 1/2 cup of crumbs with 1/2 cup finely chopped nuts for a Nut Crust.

FOR ONE 9-INCH TART SHELL
1 1/2 cups Graham crackers (about 18–20) or other
cookie crumbs
6 Tbsp butter or shortening, melted
1 to 2 Tbsp sugar (optional)

1. Put the crackers or cookies in a food processor and process 20–30 seconds until fine crumbs form. Alternatively, put them in a heavy-duty freezer bag and press into fine crumbs with a rolling pin. Pour into a bowl and stir in the butter and sugar, if using. Pour into a tart pan and press crumbs onto bottom and up sides. Chill 20 minutes.

2. Preheat oven to 375°F. Bake 6–8 minutes until set. Remove to wire rack to cool completely.

Cream Cheese Pastry

This is a moist, flaky pastry often used with sugary or nutty fillings. It is ideal for rich tartlets and tiny petits fours.

FOR ONE 9-INCH TART SHELL OR TWELVE
2- OR 3-INCH TARTLETS
1 cup all-purpose flour
1/2 tsp salt
1 tsp sugar
1/2 cup (1 stick) unsalted butter, at room temperature
4 oz full-fat cream cheese, at room temperature

1. In a large bowl, sift together the flour and salt. With an electric mixer add the butter and cream cheese and beat the ingredients together until blended and a soft dough forms. Form into a ball, flatten to a disk shape, and wrap tightly. Refrigerate about 1 hour before rolling and shaping.

Chocolate Pastry

This is a wonderfully rich, sweet pastry, almost like a chocolate cookie. It makes a stunning base for fruit tarts and tartlets and anything that goes well with chocolate.

MAKES ONE 9- OR 10-INCH TART SHELL
1/2 cup (1 stick) unsalted butter, softened
1/3 cup superfine sugar
1/2 tsp salt
2 tsp vanilla extract
1/2 cup unsweetened cocoa powder
1 1/2 cups all-purpose flour

1. Put the butter, sugar, salt and vanilla in a food processor and process 25–30 seconds until creamy. Add the cocoa and process 1 minute. Add the flour all at once and, process for 15 seconds until the flour is well-blended. Scrape dough onto a sheet of plastic wrap and shape into a flat disk. Wrap tightly and refrigerate 1 hour or overnight.

2. Soften the dough for 10 minutes at room temperature. Unwrap and turn onto a large clean piece of plastic wrap; cover with another piece of plastic wrap. Carefully roll out to about an 11-inch round about 1/4-inch thick. Peel off top sheet and invert dough into a prepared pan. Gently ease dough onto bottom and side of pan, then remove the bottom layer of plastic wrap. Press dough to the bottom and sides of pan, then roll rolling pin over the top of the pan to cut off any excess dough. Prick the base with a fork and refrigerate 1 hour.

Creamy Rice Pudding Tartlets

6–8 SERVINGS

For rice-pudding lovers, this is the ultimate recipe: a creamy orange-scented version baked in a rich sweet pastry shell—a wonderful winter dessert.

8 (3-inch) tartlets lined with Extra-Sweet Tart Crust
(p. 26), blind baked
2/3 cup Arborio (short-grain) rice
1 1/2 cups milk
1/2 cup freshly squeezed orange juice
1 tsp grated orange zest
1 cup sugar
1/2 cup heavy cream
2 eggs
2 egg yolks
2 Tbsp orange-flavored liqueur or 1 tsp vanilla extract
Confectioners' sugar for dusting, sifted
Whipped cream for serving (optional)

1. Preheat oven to 375°F. Put the rice in a medium, heavy-based saucepan with the milk. Bring to a boil over medium-high heat, reduce heat to medium-low and cook, stirring constantly, until the rice is tender and milk is absorbed, 20 minutes.

2. Stir in the orange juice, zest, and sugar and cook, stirring constantly, until the sugar is dissolved and juice is absorbed, about 5 minutes longer. Remove from heat and cool slightly.

3. Beat in the cream, eggs, egg yolks, and liqueur or vanilla extract and divide the mixture among the tartlet shells. Set on a baking sheet for easier handling. Bake until pudding mixture is just set, 15–20 minutes. Remove to a wire rack to cool. Dust with confectioners' sugar and serve warm, or cold with whipped cream if you like.

Tarte Tatin
with Crème Fraîche-Honey Swirl

8 SERVINGS

This famous French apple dessert is really an easy upside-down apple tart. The Crème Fraîche-Honey Swirl adds just the right sweet-tart accompaniment.

¾ lb bought puff pastry or 1 quantity Basic Sweet Pie Crust (p. 26)

10 Golden Delicious apples, peeled and cored
Juice of 1 lemon
6 Tbsp (¾ stick) unsalted butter
¾ cup sugar
¼ tsp ground cinnamon

CRÈME FRAÎCHE-HONEY SWIRL
1½ cups crème fraîche or sour cream
½ cup good-quality honey

1. On a lightly floured surface, roll out the pastry to an 11-inch round, ¼-inch thick. Slide onto a lightly-floured baking sheet and refrigerate until needed.

2. Halve the apples, sprinkle with lemon juice.

3. Melt the butter in a 10-inch heavy-bottomed, skillet over medium-high heat. Add the sugar and cinnamon, stirring until the sugar dissolves. Cook, stirring until a golden caramel color. Remove from heat. Do not touch the caramel—it is dangerously hot.

4. Arrange the apple halves closely in circles around the outside edge and center of the pan.

5. Return the apple-filled pan to the heat and bring to a boil. Simmer until the apples begin to soften and the caramel darkens, about 20 minutes. Remove from heat to cool slightly.

6. Preheat oven to 425°F. Soften the pastry for about 5 minutes. Slide the rolled-out dough round over the apple-filled pan, tucking the overhanging dough inside the edge. Pierce in two or three places. Bake about 25–30 minutes.

7. Prepare the crème fraîche-honey swirl: Spoon half the crème fraîche into a serving bowl. Drizzle half the honey over it, then spoon over the remaining cream and drizzle over the remaining honey. Gently draw a knife through the cream in a swirling pattern.

8. Cool the tarte tatin on a wire rack for about 5 minutes. Run a knife around the edge of the pan to release any pastry which might be stuck. Carefully unmold onto a plate and serve warm with the Crème Fraîche-Honey Swirl.

Summer Berry Strudel

6–8 SERVINGS

This is a delicious summer recipe—the almond cream adds a distinctive richness and flavor.

ALMOND CREAM
2/3 cup blanched almonds
1/4 cup sugar
2 Tbsp all-purpose flour
6 Tbsp unsalted butter, softened and cut into pieces
1 egg
1 egg yolk
1/2 tsp almond extract

FOR THE STRUDEL
3/4 cup (1 1/2 sticks) butter, melted
2 cups fresh bread crumbs
2 lb mixed summer berries, such as raspberries, blueberries, strawberries (hulled and chopped), plus extra for serving
1/2 cup sugar plus extra for sprinkling
Grated zest of 1 lemon
8 large sheets phyllo pastry
Confectioners' sugar for dusting, sifted
Whipped cream or crème fraîche for serving

1. Prepare the almond cream: Process the almonds, sugar, and flour in a food processor until finely ground. Add the butter a few pieces at a time and process until creamy. Add the egg, egg yolk, and almond extract and process until well-blended.

2. Prepare the strudel: Heat 5 tablespoons of the melted butter in a large skillet. Add the bread crumbs and stirfry for 5 minutes.

3. Preheat oven to 375°F. Grease a large baking sheet. Toss the berries in a large bowl with 1/2 cup sugar and lemon zest.

4. Place a phyllo pastry sheet onto the work surface. Brush with a little melted butter and sprinkle with about 1/4 cup of the bread crumbs. Lay a second sheet of pastry over the top, and repeat. Continue layering the remaining phyllo sheets with butter and crumbs.

5. Spread the almond cream over the stack of pastry. Spoon the berry mixture over the center and roll up jelly-roll fashion. Slide the strudel, seam-side down, onto the baking sheet. Brush with any remaining butter and sprinkle with a little sugar.

6. Bake about 45 minutes until crisp; cover with foil if it browns too quickly. Cool on a wire rack. Dust with confectioners' sugar and serve with whipped cream or crème fraîche and extra berries.

Lemon Meringue Pie

6–8 SERVINGS

This delicious old-fashioned pie is an eternal favorite. The creamy yet sharp lemon custard and the light sweet meringue combine to make an elegant dessert.

*1 (9-inch) tart shell lined with Basic Sweet Pie Crust
(p. 26), blind baked
1/3 cup cornstarch
1/8 tsp salt
11/4 cups sugar
11/2 cups water
4 eggs, separated
1 Tbsp butter, diced
Grated zest of 1 large lemon
1/2 cup freshly squeezed lemon juice (2 to 3 lemons)
1/4 tsp cream of tartar*

1. In a medium saucepan, combine the cornstarch, salt, and 3/4 cup sugar. Gradually stir in the water and bring to a boil over medium-high heat, stirring constantly until mixture is thickened; boil 1 minute more. Remove from heat.

2. Beat the egg yolks. Stir in a little of the hot cornstarch mixture, then stir the egg mixture back into the cornstarch mixture in the saucepan and return to the heat. Cook, stirring constantly and rapidly to prevent lumps, until the mixture is very thick, about 5 minutes. Remove from heat and beat in the butter, then gradually stir in the lemon zest and juice and pour into the prepared tart shell.

3. Preheat oven to 375°F. With an electric mixer, beat the egg whites and cream of tartar until soft peaks form. Gradually sprinkle in the remaining 1/2 cup sugar, a tablespoon at a time, beating well after each addition, until the whites form stiff peaks and the sugar is completely dissolved (test by rubbing a small amount between your thumb and index finger—it should feel smooth, not gritty).

4. Spoon the meringue onto the lemon mixture spreading to the edge of the crust to seal. Swirl with the back of a spoon to form a decorative pattern. Bake until meringue is just golden, 10 minutes. Transfer to a wire rack to cool completely. Serve the pie the same day.

WARNING: This recipe contains lightly cooked egg whites.

Black Bottom Tart

6–8 SERVINGS

This is an old-fashioned American pie with a new twist. Baked in a tart shell and covered with chocolate whipped cream and chocolate curls, it becomes an elegant extravaganza.

*1 (9-inch) tart shell lined with Chocolate Pastry
(p. 27), or Ginger Crumb Crust (p. 26), blind baked
2 tsp unflavored gelatin
3 Tbsp cold water
2 cups milk
2 eggs, separated
1 egg yolk
3/4 cup sugar
2 Tbsp cornstarch
2 oz bittersweet chocolate, chopped
3 to 4 Tbsp rum
1/4 tsp cream of tartar
1 cup heavy cream
Chocolate curls or grated chocolate for decoration
(optional)*

1. In a small bowl or ramekin, sprinkle the gelatin evenly over the water and set aside to soften.

2. Bring the milk to a boil. Beat the egg yolks and half the sugar until lightened, about 1 minute. Stir in the cornstarch just until blended. Pour the hot milk over the egg yolk mixture, whisking constantly.

3. Return the custard to the heat and cook, whisking constantly, until the custard thickens and boils, about 2 minutes. Remove from heat and pour 1 cup of the custard into a bowl and immediately stir in the chocolate until melted and smooth. Stir in half the rum and pour into the tart shell to set.

4. Pour the softened gelatin into the remaining custard in the saucepan and stir until dissolved. Stir in the rum and refrigerate until the mixture begins to cool and thicken slightly.

5. With an electric mixer, beat the egg whites and cream of tartar until soft peaks form. Gradually beat in the remaining sugar a tablespoon at a time, beating well after each addition until stiff peaks form. Gently fold a spoonful of whites into the setting custard, then fold in the remaining whites and spoon into the tart shell smoothing the top evenly. Refrigerate at least 2 hours until set.

6. Whip the cream and spoon over the tart making decorative swirls with the back of a spoon or knife. Decorate with chocolate curls or grated chocolate and serve chilled.

California Prune Linzer Tart

6–8 SERVINGS

This cookie-like tart is popular in Eastern Europe. Dried apricots or fresh cherries can be substituted for prunes.

12 oz ready-to-eat pitted prunes
Grated zest and juice of 1 orange
¾ cup water
2 Tbsp sugar
½ tsp ground cinnamon
½ tsp almond extract

CHOCOLATE-ALMOND PASTRY
½ cup blanched almonds
⅔ cup superfine sugar
1½ cups all-purpose flour, sifted
2 Tbsp unsweetened cocoa powder, sifted
1 tsp ground cinnamon
½ tsp salt
Grated zest of 1 orange
1 cup (2 sticks) unsalted butter, cut into pieces
2 to 3 Tbsp iced water
Confectioners' sugar for dusting, sifted

1. Bring the prunes to a boil with the orange zest and juice and water. Simmer until the liquid is absorbed and the prunes soft and plump, 15 minutes. Stir in the sugar and the cinnamon and almond extract. Process in a food processor, 20–30 seconds. Cover and chill.

2. Spray or butter an 11-inch tart pan. Process the almonds and half the sugar to fine crumbs. Add the remaining sugar, flour, cocoa, cinnamon, salt, and orange zest and process to blend. Add the butter and process until coarse crumbs form, about 20 seconds. Add the water a tablespoon at a time and process until the dough just begins to form.

3. Turn the dough onto a large piece of plastic wrap and knead lightly. Press half the dough onto the bottom and sides of the pan. Prick the bottom and refrigerate 30 minutes. Roll out the remaining dough and cut into ½-inch strips.

4. Preheat oven to 375°F. Spread the prune filling onto the pastry-lined tart pan. Arrange the dough strips on the top in a lattice pattern. Bake about 35 minutes. Cool then dust with confectioners' sugar.

Pear and Chocolate Cream Tart

6-8 SERVINGS

1 (9-inch) tart shell lined with Chocolate Pastry (p. 27)
4 oz bittersweet chocolate, melted
1 cup heavy cream
4 Tbsp sugar
1 egg
1 egg yolk
1 tsp vanilla or almond extract
3 medium ripe pears

1. In a medium saucepan over low heat, melt the chocolate, cream, and 2 tablespoons of the sugar, stirring frequently, until smooth. Remove from heat and cool slightly. Beat in the egg, egg yolk, and vanilla and set aside.

2. Preheat oven to 375°F. Peel, halve, and core the pears. Put them on a work surface cut-side down and cut crosswise into thin slices.

3. Arrange the pears spoke-fashion in the tart and press gently with your hand to carefully fan out the pear slices toward the center. Slowly pour the chocolate mixture between the pears, trying to leave the pears uncovered. Tap gently on the work surface to eliminate any air bubbles.

4. Bake 10 minutes. Reduce oven to 350°F. Sprinkle the surface of the tart with the remaining sugar and bake until the custard is set and pears are tender and glazed, about 20 minutes more. Transfer to a wire rack to cool slightly. Serve warm.

VARIATION: *one 9-inch tart shell lined with Extra-Sweet Tart Crust (p. 28). Spread with the Almond Cream from Summer Berry Strudel (p. 31). Arrange the pears as above, baking about 45 minutes until pears are tender.*

Rich Nectarine Tart

6-8 SERVINGS

This tart is equally delicious made with plums or peaches.

RICH PASTRY
1½ cups all-purpose flour
⅓ cup sugar
½ tsp ground cinnamon
½ cup butter (1 stick) at room temperature, cut into small pieces

NECTARINE FILLING
1½ lb nectarines
½ tsp almond extract
2 to 3 Tbsp sugar
2 Tbsp all-purpose flour
½ tsp ground cinnamon
¼ cup slivered almonds

1. Preheat oven to 375°F. Lightly spray or oil a 9-inch tart pan with vegetable cooking spray or oil.

2. Stir together the flour, sugar, and cinnamon. Sprinkle over the pieces of butter and, using a pastry blender, cut in the butter until a soft dough begins to form. Pour into the tart shell and, using your fingertips, press the dough evenly onto the bottom and up the sides of the pan. Set aside.

3. Cut the nectarines in half and scoop out each pit. Cut into ½-inch slices and put in a bowl. Toss the nectarines with almond extract, sugar (depending on the sweetness of fruit), flour, and cinnamon. Starting at the outside edge, arrange the slices in overlapping concentric circles and sprinkle with the almonds.

4. Set the tart shell on a baking sheet and bake until the nectarines are tender and pastry is golden and crisp, 40 minutes. Rotate the tart halfway through cooking if it begins to color unevenly. Transfer to a wire rack to cool. Serve warm.

Chocolate Profiteroles

4–6 SERVINGS

This mouthwatering dessert is served in cafés throughout France. Sometimes the profiteroles are filled with whipped or pastry cream but they are always drizzled with chocolate sauce.

FOR THE PROFITEROLES
3/4 cup all-purpose flour
1/4 tsp salt
Pinch of freshly grated nutmeg
3/4 cup water
6 Tbsp unsalted butter, cut into 6 pieces
3 eggs

CHOCOLATE SAUCE
10 oz bittersweet chocolate
8 Tbsp warm water
3 cups vanilla ice cream

1. Prepare the profiteroles: Preheat oven to 400°F and butter a large baking sheet. Sift together the flour, salt, and nutmeg. In a saucepan, bring the water and butter to a boil. Remove from heat and add the flour mixture all at once. Beat with a wooden spoon about 1 minute until well-blended and the mixture starts to pull away from the sides of the pan. Set over low heat and cook the mixture for about 2 minutes, beating constantly. Remove from heat.

2. Beat an egg in a small bowl and set aside. Add the remaining eggs, one at a time, to the flour mixture, beating well after each addition. Add the beaten egg by teaspoonfuls until the dough is smooth and shiny; it should pull away and fall slowly when dropped from a spoon.

3. Using a tablespoon, drop the dough onto the baking sheet in 12 mounds. Bake 25–30 minutes until well risen and browned. Turn off the oven and leave the puffs to cool with the oven door open.

4. Prepare the sauce: Put the chocolate and water in a small saucepan. Heat over medium heat, stirring frequently until melted and smooth. Keep warm until ready to serve, or reheat, over simmering water. Split the profiteroles in half and put a small scoop of ice cream in each. Arrange on a serving platter or divide among individual plates. Pour the chocolate sauce over the top and serve at once.

Lemon Tart

6–8 SERVINGS

1 (9- or 10-inch) tart shell lined with Extra-Sweet Tart Crust (p. 26), partially blind baked
Grated zest of 2 to 3 lemons
2/3 cup freshly squeezed lemon juice
2/3 cup sugar
1/2 cup heavy cream or crème fraîche
3 eggs
3 egg yolks
Confectioners' sugar for dusting, sifted

1. Preheat oven to 375°F. With an electric mixer on low speed, beat the lemon zest, juice, and sugar. Slowly beat in the cream or crème fraîche until well-blended, then beat in the eggs and yolks, one at a time.

2. Set the tart shell on a baking sheet for easier handling and carefully pour in the filling. (If you prefer a completely smooth filling, strain into the tart shell, removing the zest.)

3. Bake until the filling is just set, but not colored, about 20 minutes. If the tart begins to color, cover with foil. Remove to a wire rack to cool completely. Dust with confectioners' sugar before serving.

Lime Curd Phyllo Tartlets
with Raspberry Sauce

6–8 SERVINGS

These crisp phyllo cups make a stunning container for a soft tangy lime curd filling. The raspberry sauce adds a sharp color as well as flavor contrast.

4 sheets phyllo dough, defrosted if frozen
2 Tbsp unsalted butter, melted
sugar
2 eggs beaten
1/2 cup (1 stick) unsalted butter, diced
1/2 cup sugar
2 Tbsp freshly grated lime zest
1/4 cup freshly squeezed lime juice (about 2 limes)
1 lb fresh raspberries
Fresh mint sprigs for decoration (optional)

1. Preheat oven to 350°F. Lightly spray or oil four 3/4-cup custard cups or ramekins with vegetable spray or oil. Stack the phyllo dough sheets on a work surface and cut into 6-inch squares. Keep the phyllo dough covered with a damp cloth to prevent the dough from drying out.

2. Place a phyllo square on the work surface, brush with a little melted butter and sprinkle with a little sugar. Butter a second square and lay it over the first square at an angle; sprinkle with a little sugar. Repeat with two more phyllo squares, placing at different angles to create an uneven edge. Press the stack of squares into a custard cup or ramekin pressing into the edge and keeping the edges turned up. Continue to line the remaining custard cups or ramekins.

3. Set the cups on a baking sheet for easier handling and bake until crisp and golden, about 8 minutes. (Watch carefully, as the edges can burn easily.) Transfer to a wire rack and cool completely.

4. In a saucepan, combine the eggs, butter, 1⁄2 cup sugar, lime zest and juice and cook, over medium-low heat, until the mixture begins to thicken and bubbles begin to appear on the surface, about 3 minutes. Scrape into a bowl and cover with plastic wrap, pressing wrap against the surface of the curd to prevent a skin from forming. Refrigerate at least 1 hour. Stir before using.

5. Put half the raspberries and 2–3 tablespoons of sugar in a food processor and process until smooth. Strain into a bowl and stir in remaining berries. Just before serving, divide the curd mixture evenly among the phyllo cups and top each with some of the sauce; serve remaining sauce separately. Decorate with mint.

Lemon Blueberry Napoleons
with Blueberry Sauce

6–8 SERVINGS

This elegant dessert is a classic combination of puff pastry, lemon pastry cream, and sweet succulent blueberries.

BLUEBERRY SAUCE
3 cups (about 1 lb) blueberries
1⁄3 cup sugar to taste
2 to 3 Tbsp freshly squeezed lemon juice
2 to 3 Tbsp water

PASTRY CREAM
6 egg yolks
1⁄3 cup sugar
Grated zest of 1 lemon
3 Tbsp all-purpose flour
11⁄2 cups milk
1⁄2 tsp lemon or vanilla extract

1 lb bought puff pastry, defrosted if frozen
1⁄4 cup heavy cream, whipped
3 cups (about 1 lb) blueberries
Confectioners' sugar for dusting, sifted
Fresh mint sprigs for decoration (optional)

1. Prepare the sauce: Process the blueberries, sugar, lemon juice, and water in a food processor for 1 minute. Strain through a nonmetallic strainer into a bowl and taste for sweetness. Add a little more sugar if necessary. Cover and refrigerate.

2. Prepare the pastry cream: Put the yolks, sugar, and lemon zest in a bowl and whisk until creamy, about 2 minutes. Gently stir in the flour. Bring the milk to a boil. Pour half the milk over the yolk mixture, whisking vigorously. Return to the saucepan and boil for 2 minutes, whisking constantly until thickened and smooth. Stir in the lemon or vanilla extract. Remove from heat and cool.

3. Spray or brush with vegetable oil a large baking sheet. On a lightly floured surface, roll out the pastry into a rectangle at least 16 x 12 inches; cut four strips 4 inches wide and about 12 inches long. Transfer to the baking sheet. Prick with a fork and chill for about 30 minutes. Preheat oven to 400°F. Bake the pastry strips 20 minutes until crisp and golden. Cool completely on a wire rack.

4. Beat the whipped cream into the pastry cream. Spread one pastry strip with one third of the pastry cream and sprinkle with blueberries. Top with a second strip, spread with more pastry cream and blueberries. Repeat. Dust the top pastry strips with confectioners' sugar. Decorate with mint and serve with the blueberry sauce.

Pumpkin Tart
with Crunchy Walnut Topping

6–8 SERVINGS

1 (9-inch) tart shell lined with Basic Sweet Pie Crust
(p. 26), partially blind baked
1¼ cups canned pumpkin
½ cup sugar
¼ cup light brown sugar, packed
¾ cup heavy cream
⅓ cup milk
2 eggs
1 to 2 Tbsp bourbon or whiskey (optional)
¾ tsp ground cinnamon
½ tsp allspice
½ tsp ground ginger
¼ tsp ground cloves
¼ tsp ground nutmeg

TOPPING
½ cup chopped walnuts or pecans
½ cup light brown sugar, packed
2 Tbsp unsalted butter, melted
Whipped cream or vanilla ice cream for serving

1. Preheat oven to 350°F. With an electric mixer, beat the pumpkin with the remaining ingredients (except those for the topping and the whipped cream) until smooth and well-blended. Set the tart on a baking sheet for easier handling and carefully pour the mixture into the tart shell.

2. Bake until the filling is just set and the pastry is golden brown, about 45 minutes. Cover the pastry edges with a piece of foil if it browns too quickly. Carefully, remove the tart to a wire rack to cool.

3. Preheat the broiler. Combine the walnuts or pecans, sugar, and butter and sprinkle evenly over the tart. Cover the edge of the pastry with a strip of foil. Broil about 4 inches from the heat until the topping bubbles and caramelizes, watching carefully, about 1 minute. Allow to cool then serve.

Double Chocolate
Truffle Tarts

6–8 SERVINGS

A chocolate lover's fantasy: Chocolate pastry filled with rich truffle and dusted with cocoa.

8 (4-inch) tartlet pans lined with Chocolate Pastry
(p. 27), blind baked
1¼ cups heavy cream
10 oz bittersweet chocolate, chopped
2 Tbsp unsalted butter
¼ cup cognac or favorite liqueur
Unsweetened cocoa powder for dusting, sifted

1. In a medium saucepan over medium-high heat, bring the cream to a boil. Remove from heat and add the chocolate all at once, stirring until completely melted and smooth. Beat in the butter and stir in the cognac or liqueur to taste. Strain the mixture into a measuring cup or pitcher.

2. Divide the mixture evenly among the tartlet shells, smoothing the tops so they are completely flat. Refrigerate 3–4 hours or overnight.

3. Cut out strips of waxed paper about ⅜ inch wide. Place in a random pattern over each tartlet and dust with cocoa. Refrigerate until ready to serve. Allow to soften 15 minutes before serving.

Chocolate Truffle and Berry Tart
with Raspberry Cream

6-8 SERVINGS

Summer berries are the perfect foil for a rich chocolate tart shell filled with a dark chocolate and raspberry truffle mixture.

*1 (9-inch) tart shell lined with Chocolate Pastry
(p. 27), blind baked
1¾ cups heavy cream
1 cup seedless raspberry preserves
½ lb good-quality bittersweet chocolate, chopped
¼ cup Framboise or other raspberry-flavored liqueur
1½ lb mixed fresh summer berries, such as
raspberries, blackberries, strawberries (quartered
if large) or blueberries
1 cup heavy cream
1 to 2 Tbsp superfine sugar*

1. In a saucepan over medium heat, bring the cream and three quarters of the raspberry preserves to a boil, whisking to dissolve the preserves. Remove from heat and add the chocolate all at once, stirring until melted and smooth. Strain the mixture into the tart shell, tilting and turning the tart to distribute the filling evenly. Refrigerate until set, at least 1 hour.

2. In a saucepan over medium heat, heat the remaining raspberry preserves and 2 tablespoons of the liqueur until melted and bubbling. Drizzle over the berries and toss to coat well. Arrange the berries over the top. Refrigerate until ready to serve.

3. Bring to room temperature at least 30 minutes before serving. Whip the cream with the sugar and remaining liqueur until soft peaks form. Spoon into a serving bowl and serve with the tart.

Key Lime Pie
with Pineau de Charente Cream and Chocolate Sauce

6–8 SERVINGS

1 (9-inch) pie plate lined with Ginger crumb
Crust (p. 26)

KEY LIME PIE
3 large egg yolks
1 (14-oz) can sweetened condensed milk
$\frac{1}{2}$ cup Key lime or freshly squeezed lime juice (about
3 medium limes)
1 Tbsp grated lime zest

PINEAU DE CHARENTE CREAM
$1\frac{1}{4}$ cups heavy cream
$\frac{1}{4}$ cup superfine sugar
2 to 3 Tbsp Pineau de Charente or other
sweet dessert wine

CHOCOLATE SAUCE
4 oz good-quality bittersweet or semisweet chocolate,
chopped
$\frac{1}{3}$ cup heavy cream
2 to 3 Tbsp cognac or bourbon

1. Prepare the pie: With an electric mixer, beat the eggs until thick and creamy, about 3 minutes. Gradually beat in the condensed milk, lime juice and zest. Pour into the tart shell and refrigerate until completely set, at least 4 hours or overnight.

2. Prepare the Pineau de Charente cream: Beat the cream, sugar, and Pineau de Charente until stiff peaks form. Spoon the cream into a decorating bag fitted with a medium star nozzle and pipe a decorative border around the pie, near the edge of the pastry.

3. Prepare the chocolate sauce: In a small saucepan over medium-low heat, heat the chocolate and cream until melted and smooth, stirring frequently. Remove from heat and stir in the cognac.

Country-Style Peach Tart

6–8 SERVINGS

1 quantity Basic Sweet Pie Crust (p. 26)
2 lb ripe peaches
2 to 3 Tbsp lemon juice
1 Tbsp butter
3 to 4 Tbsp sugar
2 Tbsp all-purpose flour
$\frac{1}{2}$ tsp ground cinnamon
$\frac{1}{4}$ cup fresh bread crumbs, toasted or homemade
dried bread crumbs

1. Lightly spray or oil a large baking sheet. On a lightly floured surface, roll out the pastry to a 13- or 14-inch circle. Slide onto the baking sheet and refrigerate 30 minutes.

2. Peel the peaches. Cut each in half and, using a teaspoon, scoop out each pit. Cut peaches into thick slices and sprinkle with the lemon juice. Melt the butter in a large skillet over high heat. Add the peach slices and stirfry for 2–3 minutes until the peaches just begin to soften. Sprinkle in the sugar, flour, and ground cinnamon and toss to coat the peach slices well. Remove from heat and cool about 5 minutes.

3. Preheat oven to 400°F. Remove the dough from the refrigerator to soften, about 5 minutes. Sprinkle the pastry with the toasted or dried bread crumbs and spoon the peach mixture onto the dough to within 3–4 inches of the border.

4. Using your fingertips, fold and crimp the wide border of the dough over the fruit toward the center. Sprinkle with a little sugar. If the pastry cracks or is uneven, just pinch it together. Bake until crisp and golden and fruit is bubbling, about 35–40 minutes. Transfer to a wire rack to cool slightly. Serve warm or at room temperature.

Southern Pecan Tart

This all-American classic pie is delicious served warm with whipped cream, sour cream or vanilla ice cream.

1 (9-inch) tart shell, lined with Basic Sweet Pie Crust
(p. 26)
2 1/2 cups pecan halves
3 eggs
1 cup dark brown sugar, packed
1/4 cup light corn syrup
Grated zest and juice of 1/2 lemon
4 Tbsp (1/2 stick) butter, melted
1/2 tsp vanilla extract

1. Preheat oven to 350°F. Pick out about 1 cup of perfect pecan halves and set aside. Coarsely chop the remaining nuts.

2. Beat the eggs and sugar together in a large bowl. Beat in the corn syrup, grated lemon zest and juice, melted butter, vanilla extract, and the chopped pecans. Pour mixture into the tart shell and carefully set onto a baking sheet.

3. Arrange the perfect pecans in concentric circles on top of the egg-sugar mixture and bake until the filling is set and slightly puffed and pecans are well colored, about 40 minutes. Transfer to a wire rack to cool. Serve warm or at room temperature.

Coconut Custard Pie

This is a classic pie—a sweet creamy coconut filling in a tender flaky pastry crust.

1 (9-inch) pie plate lined with Basic Sweet Pie Crust
(p. 26), blind baked
2/3 cup sugar
4 Tbsp cornstarch
1/8 tsp salt
2 cups milk
3/4 cup heavy cream
3 egg yolks
2 Tbsp unsalted butter, diced
2 tsp vanilla extract
2 1/2 cups flaked sweetened coconut
1 cup heavy cream

1. In a medium saucepan, combine the sugar, cornstarch, and salt. Slowly whisk in the milk and half the cream and bring to a boil over medium heat.

2. Beat the egg yolks with the remaining cream and slowly pour into the thickened milk mixture, whisking constantly and rapidly to avoid lumps. Boil for 1 minute, whisking constantly. Remove from heat and beat in the butter, vanilla extract, and 1 1/2 cups of the coconut. Pour into the tart shell and smooth the top evenly. Cool, then refrigerate.

3. Preheat oven to 425°F. Spread the remaining coconut on a baking sheet and toast until golden, stirring occasionally, about 5 minutes. Cool the coconut completely.

4. Beat the cream until soft peaks form. Spoon into a decorating bag filled with a medium star nozzle and pipe a border of cream around the edge. Alternatively spoon cream onto the tart and swirl with the back of a spoon. Sprinkle with the toasted coconut and serve cold.

CHAPTER THREE

FRUIT
DESSERTS

Clementines
in Rosemary-Wine Sauce

8 SERVINGS

This pretty, refreshing dessert gets its unusual tang from the rosemary-scented syrup. Small tangerines or oranges can be used instead of the clementines.

ROSEMARY-WINE SYRUP
1 bottle fruity white wine
1 cup sugar
2 to 3 sprigs fresh rosemary
2 cardamom pods, lightly crushed
1 cinnamon stick
2 cloves
1 bay leaf

8 clementines or tangerines

1. Put the wine and remaining ingredients, except the clementines or tangerines, in a large, heavy-based saucepan. Bring to a boil over medium-high heat, stirring occasionally to dissolve sugar. Reduce the heat to medium-low and simmer about 20 minutes.

2. Remove the orange zest in wide strips from two clementines and add to the simmering syrup. With a sharp knife, peel all the clementines or tangerines, removing the white pith.

3. Lower the peeled fruits into the syrup and simmer for about 10 minutes, stirring gently from time to time to be sure they are well coated. Remove from heat and cool to room temperature. Transfer to a serving bowl and chill the clementines in their syrup 5–6 hours or overnight. Spoon the fruit into shallow bowls, ladle over some of the syrup and serve.

TIP: The clementines or tangerines can be prepared up to three days ahead.

Baked Pears in
Ginger Cream

4 SERVINGS

This is a simple but delicious dessert. The pears absorb the cream and have a buttery texture and sweet ginger flavor.

1¾ cups sugar
1½ cups water
1-inch piece fresh gingerroot, peeled and thinly sliced
4 large pears
1½ cups heavy cream
1 tsp vanilla extract
1 tsp ground ginger
¼ tsp ground cinnamon
1 Tbsp finely chopped preserved fresh ginger
1 Tbsp ginger syrup

1. Put 1½ cups of sugar in a large saucepan with the water and the sliced gingerroot. Bring to a boil over medium-high heat, stirring to dissolve the sugar, then reduce to a simmer.

2. Peel the pears. Cut in half lengthwise and remove the cores. Lower each pear half into the simmering syrup and poach until just tender, about 10 minutes.

3. Preheat oven to 350°F. In a bowl, whisk the cream with the remaining ¼ cup sugar, vanilla, ground ginger, cinnamon, chopped fresh ginger, and the ginger syrup.

4. Butter an ovenproof baking dish large enough to hold the pears in a single layer, and arrange the pears, cut-sides down, in the dish. Slowly spoon over the cream mixture, allowing it to seep down between the pears.

5. Bake about 40 minutes, basting the pears with the cream for the first 20 minutes, until the pears are tender when pierced with a knife and the cream is thickened and bubbling. Cool before serving.

Summer Pudding

6 SERVINGS

This is a classic English summer dessert. The lightly sweetened berries are enclosed in a layer of bread which soaks up the fruit juices. Begin at least one day ahead. Serve with additional raspberry sauce and whipped cream.

Raspberry Sauce (page 46)

PUDDING
1½ cups strawberries, cut in half
1½ cups raspberries
1½ cups blackberries
1½ cups redcurrants or blueberries
½ cup sugar
¼ cup orange juice or water
8 to 10 slices day-old, dense white bread

Extra berries for decoration
Whipped cream for serving

1. Prepare the raspberry sauce and chill until ready to serve. Prepare the pudding: Put the fruit in a large saucepan with the sugar and juice or water. Set over medium-low heat and stir occasionally until sugar dissolves and the juices begin to run. Remove from heat and turn the fruit into a colander or large strainer set over a bowl to catch the juices.

2. Lightly oil a 6 to 6½-cup bowl or basin. Trim the crusts of bread and discard. Cut each bread slice into halves or triangles. Quickly dip each slice of bread into the fruit juices and arrange the pieces juice-side out, over the base and side of the bowl to line completely. Cut any leftover pieces to fill in any gaps, so there are no spaces; trim even with the top edge of the bowl. Reserve enough slices to cover the top.

3. Spoon the fruit into the bread-lined bowl or basin and pour over any remaining fruit juices. Cover with the reserved bread pieces and any trimmings. Cover with plastic wrap and use a small plate or saucer

which just fits on top of the bowl, to sit on top of the pudding. Weight the plate with one or two heavy cans and refrigerate overnight.

4. To unmold, remove the weights, plate and plastic wrap. Run a knife blade around the edge of the pudding to separate it from the bowl and invert the pudding onto a serving plate. Holding the plate and bowl tightly together, give a firm shake to release the pudding. Carefully lift off the bowl or basin. Sprinkle a few berries over the top of the pudding and around the base. Serve with whipped cream and the raspberry sauce.

Fruity Champagne Mold
with Summer Berries

8–10 SERVINGS

This refreshing delicate dessert is perfect for a summer party. Use a variety of berries in season and, if you like, substitute a dry white wine for the champagne. If you prefer, serve with a raspberry or other fruit sauce.

2 cups sugar
1 bottle dry champagne or other sparkling
dry white wine
2 Tbsp unflavored gelatin
1 cup ripe strawberries, cut in halves or quarters
1 cup raspberries
1 cup blueberries
1 cup wild strawberries or blackberries

1. Put the sugar and champagne or wine into a medium saucepan and bring to a boil over medium-high heat, stirring to completely dissolve the sugar. Remove from heat.

2. Meanwhile, sprinkle the gelatin over cold water and allow to stand until translucent and spongy, about 5 minutes. Do not stir. Stand the bowl in a small saucepan with just simmering water and heat gently until just melted. When gelatin is completely melted, stir gently, then gradually stir into the champagne mixture.

3. Put the berries in a large bowl and pour the champagne-gelatin mixture over them. Set aside and allow to cool, but do not allow to set. Rinse a 6-cup mold or loaf pan with cold water and spoon in half the liquid and fruits. Refrigerate until set; keep the remaining mixture at room temperature. When the first layer is set, carefully spoon over the remaining fruits and liquid; refrigerate until set, 4–6 hours or overnight. Cover the mold or loaf pan tightly with plastic wrap.

4. To unmold, dip the bottom half of the mold into warm water for 2–3 seconds; wipe dry. Run a sharp knife around the edge to break the air lock. Place a serving dish over the mold and, holding them tightly together, invert them quickly with a firm shake; the dessert should drop onto the plate. If not, rest a hot cloth on the bottom of the inverted mold for 2–3 seconds and try again. Carefully lift off the mold, wipe any drips, and refrigerate immediately to reset the surface.

5. To serve, dip a thin-bladed knife into hot water, wipe dry. Cut the dessert into slices and transfer to dessert plates. If you like, serve with a raspberry or other fruit sauce.

_____

TIP: To melt gelatin in the microwave: Soften as above, then microwave on High (100% power) at 10–15 second intervals until completely melted; stir. (Do not allow to boil rapidly as this will inhibit its setting properties.)

Vanilla Poached Pears
with Vanilla Custard

---

6 SERVINGS

The flavor of real vanilla is exquisite and goes well with the tender pears and the custard.

VANILLA POACHED PEARS
3/4 cup sugar
1 vanilla bean
2 cups water
6 ripe pears
lemon juice

VANILLA BEAN CUSTARD SAUCE
1 vanilla bean
2 1/2 cups milk
9 egg yolks
1/4 cup sugar

Slivered toasted almonds or filberts, for decoration
(optional)

1. Put the sugar in a large saucepan. Split the vanilla bean lengthwise with a sharp knife, scrape the seeds into the saucepan and add the split bean. Add the water and cook until the sugar has dissolved.

2. Peel the pears, rubbing each with a little lemon juice. Core each pear from the bottom, leaving the stem end intact. Cut a thin slice from the bottom of each pear to make a flat bottom. Lower into the sugar syrup and add enough water to cover.

3. Cut out a circle of waxed or greaseproof paper and cover the top of the pears; cover the saucepan. Simmer for 20 minutes until tender. Remove from heat and cool the pears in the syrup.

4. Remove the pears to a large serving bowl with a slotted spoon. Bring the syrup to a boil. Boil rapidly for about 10 minutes to reduce by about half. Strain over the reserved pears and cool completely. Cover and refrigerate for several hours or overnight.

5. Prepare the custard: Split the vanilla bean as in step 1 and bring to a boil in a medium heavy-based saucepan with the milk. Beat the egg yolks with the sugar until pale and thick. Pour the hot milk over the egg yolk mixture, whisking constantly. Return to the saucepan and cook over low heat until the sauce thickens and coats the back of a wooden spoon, stirring constantly. (Do not boil or the sauce will curdle.) Strain into a bowl and cool completely. Cover and refrigerate.

6. Serve each pear with some of its syrup. Spoon some custard over each and sprinkle with a few toasted slivered almonds or filberts.

Apricot-Glazed Berries
with Mascarpone Cream

6–8 SERVINGS

Summer berries make an ideal summer fruit dessert. Keep them simple with this easy glaze and serve with a luscious mascarpone cream.

MASCARPONE CREAM
9 oz mascarpone* (Italian cream cheese),
at room temperature
1/2 cup heavy cream
2 tsp sugar
2 Tbsp cognac or orange-flavored liqueur
1 tsp vanilla extract
2 egg whites

GLAZED BERRIES
1 1/2 lb mixed fresh berries such as strawberries
(halved if large), raspberries, blackberries, and
blueberries
3 Tbsp light brown sugar
3 Tbsp apricot preserves
1/3 cup cognac or orange-flavored liqueur
1/2 cup toasted slivered almonds or filberts

1. Prepare the mascarpone cream: With an electric mixer, beat the mascarpone, cream, and sugar until smooth and well-blended, 1–2 minutes. Beat in the cognac or orange-flavored liqueur and vanilla. In another bowl with cleaned beaters, beat the egg whites until soft peaks form; beat 30 seconds longer. Stir a spoonful of egg whites into the cream mixture to lighten it, then fold in the remaining egg whites until just blended. Spoon into a serving bowl and refrigerate, covered, until ready to serve.

2. Put the berries in a large serving bowl and toss lightly to mix; set aside. Put the brown sugar, apricot preserves, and cognac or orange-flavored liqueur in a small saucepan and bring to a boil over medium heat, stirring to blend. Slowly drizzle the glaze over the berries and sprinkle with the toasted almonds or filberts. Allow to stand at room temperature for at least 1 hour before serving with the cream.

*Mascarpone is an Italian cream cheese available in large supermarkets and gourmet shops.

**This dessert contains uncooked egg whites.

Caramelized Apple Charlotte
with Lemon Crème Anglaise

6 SERVINGS

This is a classic dessert. A tangy apple purée is encased in a buttery bread crust which caramelizes as it bakes. The Lemon Crème Anglaise makes a perfect accompaniment.

CREME ANGLAISE
2½ cups milk
1 large lemon
8 egg yolks
¼ cup sugar

APPLE CHARLOTTE
2½ lb sharp-flavored dessert apples
2 Tbsp water
2 Tbsp lemon juice
⅔ cup light brown sugar, packed
1 tsp ground cinnamon
½ tsp freshly ground nutmeg
6 Tbsp unsalted butter, melted
Sugar for sprinkling
7 to 8 slices dense white bread

1. Put the milk in a heavy-based medium saucepan. Remove the zest from the lemon in wide strips, add to the milk in the pan, and bring to a boil.

2. With an electric mixer, beat the egg yolks and sugar until thick, about 3 minutes. Whisk in the hot milk and return the mixture to the saucepan. Cook the sauce until it begins to thicken and coats the back of a wooden spoon, stirring constantly. (Do not allow to boil or it will curdle.) Strain into a chilled bowl, cool, and refrigerate.

3. Peel the apples. Quarter, core, and cut into thick slices. Put the apple slices, water, and lemon juice in a skillet and cook for about 15 minutes until the apples are very soft. Add the sugar, cinnamon, and nutmeg and cook until the apples are almost puréed and all the liquid has evaporated.

4. Preheat oven to 400°F. Brush a 6-cup charlotte mold or soufflé dish with a little melted butter and line the bottom with nonstick baking parchment. Butter again and sprinkle with sugar. Trim the crusts from the bread slices and brush one side with the melted butter. Cut two of the bread slices into triangles and use to line the base of the dish, buttered-side down, making sure there are no spaces. Use more bread to line the sides of the dish, buttered-side out, leaving no gaps.

5. Spoon in the apple purée and cover the top with any remaining bread slices, buttered-side up.

6. Bake for 20 minutes; reduce the oven temperature to 350°F and bake 25 minutes more until browned and crisp. Unmold and serve with the custard.

Peach Melba

6 SERVINGS

The great French chef August Escoffier created this now famous dessert for the opera singer Dame Nellie Melba. It's a wonderful combination of poached peaches, vanilla ice cream, and raspberry sauce.

POACHED PEACHES
1/4 cup sugar
1 vanilla bean, split lengthwise
2 to 3 strips orange zest
Juice of 1 orange
4 cups water
3 large ripe peaches

RASPBERRY SAUCE
1 lb fresh or frozen raspberries
1 Tbsp lemon juice
2 to 3 Tbsp sugar
2 Tbsp raspberry-flavored liqueur (optional)
Vanilla ice cream for serving

1. Put the sugar in a large saucepan, with the split vanilla bean, orange zest strips, orange juice, and the water. Bring to a boil, stirring occasionally until the sugar dissolves.

2. Cut peaches in half lengthwise and remove pits. Lower peaches into poaching syrup, cut-side down, and press a piece of waxed paper against surface. Cover and simmer 12–15 minutes, until tender. Cool in the syrup.

3. Remove peaches from their syrup and peel off skins. Drain on paper towels (reserve the syrup for another use). Cover and refrigerate for several hours or overnight.

4. Prepare the raspberry sauce: Place raspberries, lemon juice, and sugar in a food processor fitted with a metal blade. Process 1 minute. Press through a fine sieve into a small bowl, stir in the raspberry liqueur, and refrigerate 1–2 hours until well chilled.

5. To serve, place a peach half, cut-side up on a dessert plate, fill with a scoop of vanilla ice cream and spoon the raspberry sauce over the ice cream.

Tropical Fruit Salad
with Coconut-Flavored Thai Cream

6 SERVINGS

If fresh coconut milk is unavailable, use a 13½-oz can of coconut milk diluted with ⅔ cup water.

COCONUT MILK
1 large heavy coconut
2 cups boiling water

COCONUT-FLAVORED THAI CREAM
3 Tbsp sugar
¼ cup canned cream of coconut
6 cardamom pods, lightly crushed
2 stalks fresh lemon grass*, trimmed and bruised
2-inch piece fresh gingerroot, peeled and sliced
2 star anise*
1 vanilla bean, split lengthwise

5 cups chopped tropical fruits, such as mango, papaya, melon, peach, banana, kiwi, peeled lychees, and starfruit
½ cup fresh raspberries
Mint sprigs for decoration (optional)

1. Using a screwdriver, pierce the three "eyes" of the coconut and drain the liquid into a bowl. (Reserve for another use.) Put the coconut in a heavy-duty freezer bag and twist lightly to close. Using a hammer or back of a cleaver, strike the coconut to break the shell in several places. Remove pieces from the bag and, using a small sharp knife, separate the flesh from the "hairy" brown shell. Remove the brown skin with a vegetable peeler or small sharp knife. Cut the coconut flesh into small pieces.

2. Fit a food processor with a fine shredding disc and with the machine running drop the pieces through the feed tube to shred. Turn the shredded coconut into a bowl. Put the shredded coconut into the processor and, with the machine running, pour the boiling water through the feed tube; process about 30 seconds. Pour back into the bowl and allow to cool until just warm.

3. In small batches, press the coconut mixture through a fine sieve set over a large mixing bowl; press very hard extracting as much liquid as possible; this is the coconut milk. You should be able to extract about 2 cups.

4. Put the coconut milk, sugar, cream of coconut, cardamom pods, lemon grass, gingerroot, star anise, and vanilla bean in a large saucepan and bring to a simmer. Cool completely, then refrigerate overnight. Strain into a large measuring cup or pitcher and discard the spices.

5. To serve, arrange the fruit in a large shallow serving bowl. Pour over the chilled coconut cream, sprinkle with the raspberries and decorate with fresh mint sprigs.

*Lemon grass can be found in large supermarkets or Oriental grocers. Star anise is available in large supermarkets or Chinese or Oriental specialty grocers.

Fresh Strawberries
with Grand Marnier Sabayon

4 SERVINGS

A sabayon is like a hot mousse made with flavored sweetened egg yolks which are lightly cooked. This sauce is delicious over any fruit.

GRAND MARNIER SABAYON
3 egg yolks
2 Tbsp sugar
1⁄2 cup white wine
3 Tbsp Grand Marnier or other orange-flavored liqueur

STRAWBERRIES
11⁄2 lb fresh strawberries
1 tsp lemon juice
1 Tbsp Grand Marnier or other orange-flavored liqueur
Confectioners' sugar for dusting, sifted

Toasted, slivered almonds for decoration

1. Prepare the sabayon: Put the egg yolks, sugar, wine, and liqueur into the top of a double boiler or heatproof bowl and whisk to blend. Set the top of the double boiler or heatproof bowl over the bottom half of saucepan of simmering water. With an electric mixer, over the heat, beat until the mixture thickens and lightens in color and the beaters leave a trail on the bottom of the bowl, about 10 minutes. Remove from heat and continue beating until mixture cools slightly. Set aside, but keep warm.

2. Prepare the strawberries: Hull the berries and brush clean (try not to wash). Slice each berry lengthwise and, in a bowl, toss with the lemon juice and liqueur. Dust with confectioners' sugar.

3. Arrange the strawberries in individual serving dishes and spoon over the sabayon. Sprinkle with toasted slivered almonds and serve immediately.

Peaches and Cream
Meringues

8 SERVINGS

The crunchy meringues are filled with mascarpone, whipped cream, and lightly poached peaches—an elegant combination for any special occasion.

POACHED PEACHES
1⁄2 cup sugar
1⁄2 cinnamon stick
2 strips lemon zest
3 cups water
4 ripe peaches

MERINGUES
3 egg whites
1⁄4 tsp cream of tartar
3⁄4 cup superfine sugar
1 tsp vanilla extract

MASCARPONE CREAM
11⁄4 cups heavy cream
2 Tbsp Amaretto liqueur
4 oz mascarpone
1⁄4 cup superfine sugar

Toasted pine nuts (pignoli) for decoration

1. Put the sugar, cinnamon stick, lemon zest, and water into a saucepan large enough to hold the peaches. Bring to a boil, stirring until sugar dissolves. Lower the peaches into the syrup. Simmer for 10 minutes. Cool in the syrup.

2. Remove peaches from the syrup and skin. Cut each peach in half, and remove the pit. Slice the halves and put into a bowl. Bring the syrup back to a boil and boil rapidly until reduced and syrupy, about 10 minutes. Strain over the peach slices and cool. Refrigerate.

3. Preheat oven to 275°F. Line a large baking sheet with nonstick baking parchment. Beat the egg whites until frothy. Add the cream of tartar and beat until stiff peaks just begin to form. Gradually sprinkle over about three-quarters of the sugar, beating well after each addition until stiff and glossy. Fold in the remaining sugar and vanilla extract.

4. Spoon the mixture into eight small circles onto the baking sheet, making a well in the center of each.

5. Bake about 40 minutes until set. Turn off the oven and leave in the oven 45 minutes longer to dry out. Remove meringues to a wire rack to cool.

6. Prepare the mascarpone cream: Beat the cream with the Amaretto until soft peaks form. Beat the mascarpone with the sugar until smooth. Beat a spoonful of cream into the mascarpone mixture to lighten it, then fold in the remaining cream.

7. Fill each meringue with a spoonful of the cream. Arrange the peach slices on top, spooning a little extra syrup around the meringue. Sprinkle with a few toasted pine nuts.

Sautéed Bananas with Caribbean Rum Sauce

4 SERVINGS

This is a fantastic combination of bananas with those Caribbean flavors that go so well together—lime, pineapple, brown sugar, and rum; especially delicious with coconut or vanilla ice cream.

CARIBBEAN RUM SAUCE
1/2 cup sugar
1/2 cup dark brown sugar, packed
1/3 cup water
15 1/2-oz can crushed pineapple with its own juice
Grated zest and juice of 1 lime
3 Tbsp unsalted butter
2 Tbsp dark rum

2 Tbsp unsalted butter
4 bananas
4 kumquats, thinly sliced (optional)
1/4 cup dark rum

Vanilla or coconut ice cream for serving
Mint sprigs for decoration

1. Prepare the sauce: Put all the ingredients for the sauce except the rum in a medium saucepan and bring to a boil over medium heat, stirring frequently to dissolve the sugar. Simmer gently until reduced and thickened, about 7 minutes. Remove from heat, stir in the rum and keep warm.

2. In a large skillet, melt the butter over medium-high heat. Peel the bananas and cut in half lengthwise. When the butter has stopped bubbling and is very hot, add the bananas. Cook about 5 minutes, turning once halfway through cooking, until soft and just tender. Sprinkle over the kumquats if using, and carefully pour in the rum. With a long match and tilting the pan, ignite the rum. Shake the pan to distribute the rum and remove from heat.

3. Scoop the vanilla or coconut ice cream into four large dessert dishes. Divide the banana mixture evenly around the ice cream and spoon over the warm Caribbean rum sauce. Decorate each serving with a few sprigs of mint.

TIP: The sauce can be made up to three days ahead, then gently reheated before serving.

CHAPTER FOUR

FROZEN DESSERTS

Chocolate Marquise
with Espresso Crème Anglaise

8–10 SERVINGS

MARQUISE
8 oz good-quality bittersweet or semisweet chocolate,
chopped
5 Tbsp unsalted butter, softened
4 large eggs, separated
2 Tbsp cognac or dark rum
1/4 tsp cream of tartar

ESPRESSO CRÈME ANGLAISE
2 1/2 cups milk
1 1/2 Tbsp instant espresso coffee powder, dissolved in
2 Tbsp hot water
9 egg yolks
1/4 cup of sugar
1 to 2 Tbsp coffee-flavored liqueur (optional)
1 tsp vanilla extract

1. Line a 5-cup terrine or 8 x 4-inch loaf pan with
plastic wrap, smoothing out all the wrinkles.

2. Heat the chocolate and butter until melted.
Remove from heat and beat in yolks, one at a time;
add the cognac.

3. Beat the egg whites until frothy. Add the cream of
tartar and beat until the whites form soft peaks, beat
30 seconds longer. Fold the whites into the chocolate
mixture. Spoon into the terrine smoothing the top.
Cover and freeze overnight.

4. Prepare the sauce: Bring the milk to a boil with
the coffee mixture. Beat egg yolks and sugar until
thick and creamy, 2–3 minutes. Whisk in the hot milk
and return to the heat. Cook until thickened. (Do not
boil or it will curdle.) Strain and stir in the coffee
liqueur, if using, and vanilla. Cool then refrigerate.

5. Invert the marquise onto a serving dish. Remove
the plastic wrap. Serve in thin slices with a little
espresso crème anglaise.

Nectarine and Mango
Ice Cream

6–8 SERVINGS

1 cup water
1 cup sugar, plus 2 to 3 Tbsp
1 vanilla bean, split in half lengthwise
5 ripe nectarines
1 large ripe mango
Juice of 3 ripe passionfruit or 1 orange, strained
2 cups heavy cream

1. Put the water and 1 cup sugar in a saucepan.
Scrape the seeds from the vanilla bean into the
saucepan. Bring to a boil over medium-high heat,
stirring to dissolve the sugar. Score the bottom of
each nectarine and lower into the syrup. Simmer
gently, 10 minutes, until very tender (the time will
depend on the ripeness of the fruit). Remove from
heat and cool.

2. Peel the mango. Cut down both sides of the
center stone to remove as much flesh as possible; cut
into pieces. Scrape off any flesh still attached to the
stone. Set aside.

3. Remove the nectarines from the syrup and
remove and discard the skins. Cut each nectarine in
half and remove the pit. Put the nectarine halves in a
food processor. Add 1 cup of the syrup, the mango
pieces and the passionfruit or orange juice and
process until a smooth purée forms. Remove three
quarters of a cup of purée. Taste for sweetness and
add more sugar if necessary. Chill until ready to
serve. Add the cream and 2 to 3 tablespoons of sugar
to the processor and blend. Taste and add more
sugar if necessary.

4. Pour the mixture into an ice-cream maker and
freeze as the manufacturer directs. Transfer to a
freezerproof container and freeze 3–4 hours until
firm. Serve with the fruit purée.

Bitter Chocolate Sorbet
with Tangerine Sauce

6–8 SERVINGS

SORBET
1 cup sugar
2 cups water
5 oz (5 squares) unsweetened chocolate, chopped
4 oz good-quality semisweet chocolate, chopped

TANGERINE SAUCE
Segments of 2 tangerines
Grated zest of 2 tangerines
1½ cups freshly squeezed tangerine juice
¼ cup sugar or to taste
2 tsp cornstarch dissolved in 2 tsp cold water

1. Prepare the sorbet: Put the sugar and water in a saucepan and bring to a boil over medium-high heat, stirring to dissolve the sugar. Boil for 2 minutes.

2. Put the chocolate in a food processor. Process for 30 seconds until finely chopped.

3. With the machine running, pour the boiling syrup over the chocolate. Allow the machine to continue running 1–2 minutes until chocolate is completely melted and mixture is smooth.

4. Strain chocolate mixture into a large measuring pitcher or bowl and cool completely, then refrigerate until chilled, stirring occasionally. Transfer to an ice-cream maker and freeze as the manufacturer directs. Spoon into a container and freeze 2 hours or overnight.

5. Prepare the sauce: Put the tangerine segments in a bowl and set aside. Bring the tangerine zest, juice, and sugar to a boil over medium-high heat; boil 2 minutes. Whisk the cornstarch into the boiling juice mixture until thickened, simmer 1 minute. Pour into the bowl with tangerine segments. Cool, stirring from time to time. Chill.

6. Soften the sorbet for 10 minutes. Spoon a little tangerine sauce over each serving.

Celebration Brownie-
Baked Alaska

12–14 SERVINGS

This spectacular-looking dessert is ideal for a party, as it can be prepared well ahead of time and baked just before serving. Any combination of ice cream flavors can be used, but the ones below work beautifully.

BROWNIE LAYER
½ cup (1 stick) unsalted butter
2 squares (2 oz) unsweetened chocolate, chopped
1 cup of sugar
2 eggs
1 tsp vanilla extract
½ cup all-purpose flour
½ cup pecans, chopped and toasted

FILLING
1 pt Rich Chocolate Ice Cream (p.57) or other good-quality chocolate ice cream
1 pt good-quality vanilla ice cream
1 pt good-quality raspberry sherbet

MERINGUE TOPPING
4 egg whites
1/4 tsp cream of tartar
1 cup sugar
2 tsp vanilla extract
Fresh raspberry sauce (p. 46) to serve (optional)

1. Preheat the oven to 350°F. Lightly grease an 8-inch cake pan. Line the bottom with nonstick baking parchment or waxed paper; regrease and dust lightly with flour.

2. Melt the butter and chocolate. Stir in sugar, eggs, and vanilla extract. Stir in the flour and pecans. Spoon into the pan.

3. Bake about 25 minutes. Remove to wire rack to cool briefly, then invert onto the rack to cool completely. Wrap tightly until ready for use.

4. Line a 6- to 8-cup freezerproof mixing bowl with a diameter of not more than 8 inches with plastic wrap, allowing enough wrap to fold over bottom when filled. Freeze while softening the chocolate ice cream, about 20 minutes.

5. Spread the softened chocolate ice cream with an even 1-inch layer around the bowl to within about 1/2-inch of top edge of bowl. Cover and freeze 30 minutes. Soften the white chocolate ice cream, about 20 minutes.

6. Remove the bowl from the freezer. Spread the softened white chocolate ice cream against the chocolate layer about 1-inch thick. Cover, then refreeze about 30 minutes. Soften the sherbet.

7. Fill the center of the bowl with the raspberry sherbet. Place the brownie layer onto the surface of the ice-cream filled bowl pressing firmly against the surface; trim to fit if necessary. Fold the excess plastic wrap over the top of bowl and freeze overnight.

8. Prepare the topping: Preheat oven to 450°F. Beat the egg whites and cream of tartar until stiff peaks form. Gradually add the sugar, 2 tablespoons at a time, beating well after each addition, until stiff and glossy. Beat in the vanilla. Spoon into a large decorating bag fitted with a medium star nozzle.

9. Remove the ice-cream filled bowl from the freezer and peel back the plastic wrap. Invert the bowl onto a broiler-proof serving dish and remove remaining plastic wrap. Starting at the center of the top, pipe vertical stripes of rosettes or scrolls with edges touching, around side of dessert. Pipe a border around the bottom edge to seal completely. (The dessert can be frozen at this stage for several hours.) Bake 3–5 minutes until golden and set.

Caramel Crunch Ice Cream in Cookie Cups

6–8 SERVINGS

CARAMEL CRUNCH ICE CREAM
1/2 cup blanched almonds
1 cup sugar
1/4 cup water
2 cups milk
6 eggs yolks
1 cup heavy cream

COOKIE CUPS
1/2 cup whole blanched almonds, lightly toasted
1/2 cup superfine sugar
3 Tbsp unsalted butter, softened
2 egg whites
1/2 tsp almond extract
1/4 cup all-purpose flour, sifted

CARAMEL SAUCE
1 1/3 cups sugar
1 1/4 cups water

1. Prepare the ice cream: Lightly oil a cookie sheet. Place the almonds in a saucepan with 1/3 cup of sugar, sprinkle with the water, and bring to a boil. Boil without stirring 4–5 minutes until syrup is a caramel color and nuts begin to pop. Immediately pour out onto the cookie sheet. Do not touch—caramel is dangerously hot. Cool completely.

2. Break the mixture into pieces and place in a food processor. Process to fine crumbs.

3. Bring the milk to a boil. Beat the egg yolks and remaining sugar 2–3 minutes until thick. Whisk the hot milk into the egg mixture and cook about 3–4 minutes until the mixture thickens and coats the back of the spoon.

4. Strain and cool. Refrigerate until chilled, then stir in the cream and caramel-nut mixture. Transfer to an ice-cream maker and freeze as manufacturer directs. Spoon into a container and freeze overnight.

5. Prepare the cookie cups: Preheat oven to 400°F. Butter two baking sheets. Process the almonds and 2 tablespoons of the sugar until fine crumbs form. With an electric mixer, beat the butter until creamy. Add remaining sugar and beat 1 minute until fluffy. Gradually beat in the egg whites and almond extract. Sift the flour over the butter mixture and fold in, then fold in almond-sugar mixture.

6. Drop the mixture by tablespoons 8 inches apart onto prepared baking sheets. With the back of a wet spoon, spread each mound into a thin 4-inch round.

7. Bake one sheet at a time, about 4–5 minutes. Remove to a wire rack and, quickly transfer each to an upturned drinking glass, pressing over the bottom to form a fluted basket. Allow to set; continue with remaining batter.

8. Prepare the caramel sauce: Cook the sugar and half the water. Boil without stirring 4–5 minutes until a golden caramel color. Remove from heat and, standing back from pan, pour in remaining water. Cook 1–2 minutes until caramel dissolves. Cool (do not refrigerate).

9. Soften the ice cream 15–20 minutes then fill each cup. Drizzle with a little caramel sauce.

Frozen Peanut Butter Fudge Torte

10–12 SERVINGS

Chocolate and peanut butter is a well-loved combination. It works especially well in this rich do-ahead summer dessert.

PEANUT-CHOCOLATE CRUMB CRUST

8 oz chocolate wafers (about 24–26)
1/2 cup dry roasted peanuts, finely chopped and toasted
1/4 cup (1/2 stick) unsalted butter, melted

FUDGE FILLING

1/2 cup heavy cream
3 Tbsp light corn syrup
5 oz semisweet chocolate, chopped
1 Tbsp vanilla extract

ICE CREAM LAYER

3 pts good-quality chocolate ice cream or Rich Chocolate Ice Cream (p. 57)
3/4 cup dry roasted peanuts, chopped and toasted
1 1/2 cups smooth peanut butter
3/4 cup honey
1 cup heavy cream
1/4 cup superfine sugar
1 tsp vanilla extract

1. Prepare the crumb crust: Lightly spray or oil a 9-inch springform pan. Put the chocolate wafers and peanuts in a food processor and process to fine crumbs. Pour in the butter and process until blended. Pat onto the bottom and up sides of the pan.

2. Prepare the filling: Bring the cream and corn syrup to a boil. Remove from heat and add the chocolate, stirring until melted and smooth. Stir in the vanilla; set aside until cooled, stirring occasionally. Pour into the crumb-lined pan. Cool completely.

3. Soften the ice cream 15–20 minutes until spreadable. Put the chopped nuts, peanut butter, and honey in a bowl and stir. Add the ice cream scoop by scoop and, with an electric mixer on low speed, beat in the ice cream. Do not allow the ice cream to melt completely. Spoon onto the fudge layer and smooth the top. Freeze 4–6 hours or overnight.

4. To assemble: Soften 5 minutes at room temperature. Run a knife around the edge of the pan to loosen, then remove the side of the pan. With an electric mixer, beat the cream with the sugar and

vanilla until stiff peaks form. Spoon into a medium decorating bag fitted with a medium star nozzle and pipe cream in a lattice or other design across the top of the torte and around the edge. Serve immediately or freeze until ready to serve. Soften 5–10 minutes at room temperature before serving.

Pink Grapefruit and Campari Granita

6–8 SERVINGS

A granita is a kind of sorbet with a coarse, grainy texture. It makes an ideal dessert after a rich meal or a super refresher at a summer barbecue or outdoor meal.

1/2 cup sugar
1/2 cup water
3 cups pink grapefruit juice, strained
1/2 cup Campari
Fresh pink grapefruit sections for serving

1. Put the sugar and water into a medium saucepan and bring to a boil over medium-high heat, stirring frequently until sugar dissolves. Boil for 3 minutes, remove from heat and cool. Stir in grapefruit juice and Campari and pour into a 13 x 9 x 1-inch baking dish or shallow plastic container.

2. Place the dish or container in the freezer and freeze until partially frozen, about 2 hours. Stir in the mixture occasionally bringing the frozen crystals from the edge into the center. Freeze overnight (at least 6–8 hours).

3. To serve: Using the tines of a fork, scrape the mixture into large flakes and spoon into chilled glasses. Top with a few pink grapefruit sections and serve immediately.

Mango Lime Sorbet
with Mango and Lime Syrup

6–8 SERVINGS

LIME SYRUP
1/2 cup sugar
1/2 cup water
3 limes
1 tsp arrowroot

MANGO-LIME SORBET
1 cup sugar
1 cup water
3 very ripe mangoes
Grated zest of 1 lime
1/3 cup fresh lime juice
2 Tbsp vodka

Fresh mango slices for serving
Mint sprigs for decoration

1. Prepare the syrup: Put the sugar and water into a medium saucepan and bring to a boil over medium-high heat, stirring occasionally until sugar dissolves.

2. Peel the zest from one lime. Stack two to three pieces of zest at a time and, using a sharp knife, cut into very thin julienne strips. Repeat with all the strips then add them to the syrup and simmer about 10 minutes.

3. Squeeze the juice from the three limes and stir into the arrowroot until dissolved. Stir into the simmering syrup and bring to a boil. Boil 1 minute until the syrup thickens slightly and becomes clear again. Remove from heat and cool, stirring occasionally. Cover and refrigerate until well chilled.

4. Prepare the sorbet: Put the sugar and water into a saucepan and bring to a boil over medium-high heat, stirring occasionally until sugar dissolves. Simmer 5 minutes, remove from heat and cool.

5. Peel the mangoes. Cut down both sides of the center stone to remove as much flesh as possible and process to a fine purée in a food processor. Add the lime zest and juice and process to blend.

6. Stir the purée into the warm sugar-syrup and stir in the vodka. Refrigerate until chilled then transfer to an ice-cream maker and freeze as the manufacturer directs. Spoon into a container and freeze.

7. Soften the sorbet 10 minutes. Put one or two scoops into a dish, top with mango slices and spoon over a little lime syrup. Decorate with mint.

Blood Orange Ice Cream
with Bitter Chocolate Sauce

8–10 SERVINGS

BITTER CHOCOLATE SAUCE
3 Tbsp sugar
1/2 cup water
6 oz good-quality bittersweet chocolate
(70% cocoa solids), chopped
2 Tbsp unsalted butter
4 Tbsp heavy cream
2 Tbsp orange-flavored liqueur

ICE CREAM
Finely grated zest of 3 blood oranges
Juice of 5 blood oranges
Juice of 2 passionfruit or orange, strained
3/4 cup superfine sugar
4 egg yolks, lightly beaten
4 to 6 cardamon pods, crushed
1 1/4 cups heavy cream

1. Prepare the sauce: Put the sugar and water in a medium saucepan and bring to a boil, stirring to dissolve the sugar. Stir in the chocolate and butter. Remove from heat, stirring until melted and smooth.

Stir in the cream and orange-flavored liqueur. Pour into a bowl and cool, stirring from time to time. Serve warm or at room temperature.

2. Prepare the ice cream: Put the grated zest, orange juice, passionfruit or orange juice, sugar, and egg yolks in a medium, heavy-bottomed saucepan and set over low heat. Cook, stirring constantly using a wooden spoon, until the mixture thickens slightly and coats the back of the spoon. (Do not overheat or the mixture may curdle.) Pour into a bowl and allow to cool, stirring from time to time. If you prefer a smoother ice cream with no zest, strain into the bowl. Stir in the cream and cover; refrigerate until cold.

3. Transfer to an ice-cream maker and freeze as manufacturer directs. Spoon into a container or bowl and freeze until firm, 3–4 hours or overnight. To serve, pour a little chocolate sauce into a shallow bowl and arrange 1–2 scoops of ice cream on top.

Chocolate-Coffee Ice Cream Sundae
with Rich Chocolate Ice Cream

6–8 SERVINGS

The main feature of this fabulous ice cream sundae is the rich homemade chocolate ice cream—well worth making.

RICH CHOCOLATE ICE CREAM
8 oz bittersweet chocolate, chopped
2 cups half-and-half or half milk and half light cream
3 egg yolks
1⁄4 cup sugar
1 1⁄2 cups heavy cream
1 Tbsp vanilla extract

COFFEE CREAM
3 Tbsp instant coffee powder or granules, dissolved in
3 Tbsp boiling water, cooled
1 1⁄2 cups heavy cream
2 Tbsp coffee-flavored liqueur

CHOCOLATE COFFEE SAUCE
1 1⁄4 cups heavy cream
2 Tbsp instant coffee powder or granules, dissolved in
2 Tbsp boiling water
11 oz bittersweet chocolate, chopped
2 Tbsp coffee-flavored liqueur

1. Prepare the ice cream: Melt the chocolate with 1⁄2 cup of the half-and-half until smooth.

2. Bring remaining half-and-half to a boil. With an electric mixer, beat the egg yolks and sugar until thick and creamy, 2–3 minutes. Gradually pour hot milk over yolks, whisking constantly, and return mixture to saucepan.

3. Cook until custard thickens and coats the back of a wooden spoon, stirring constantly. (Do not allow to boil or custard will curdle.) Stir into the melted chocolate until blended.

4. Pour the cold cream into a large bowl and strain custard into bowl with the cream. Blend, cool, and refrigerate. Transfer to an ice-cream maker and freeze as manufacturer directs.

5. Prepare the coffee cream: Stir the dissolved coffee into the cream. With an electric mixer, beat the cream until it holds soft peaks. Beat in the coffee liqueur. Spoon into a decorating bag fitted with a medium star nozzle and refrigerate.

6. Prepare the sauce: Bring the cream and dissolved coffee to a boil. Remove from heat and add the chocolate all at once and stir until melted. Stir in the liqueur and strain into a bowl. Keep warm.

7. Allow the ice cream to soften 15–20 minutes. Pipe a layer of coffee cream into the bottom of six wine goblets. Add two to three scoops of chocolate ice cream and top with a rosette of coffee cream. Spoon over a little warm chocolate sauce.

Frozen Chocolate-Coated Banana Pops

MAKES 6

These chocolate-coated bananas-on-a-stick are popular with adults and children alike.

3 ripe bananas
8 oz bittersweet or semisweet chocolate, chopped
3 Tbsp vegetable shortening
1⁄2 cup unsalted peanuts, finely chopped

1. Line a small cookie sheet with waxed paper. Peel bananas, being sure to remove all stringy fibers. Cut each banana in half crosswise, then insert a wooden pop-type stick 1½-inches into the cut end of each banana half. Place on a lined cookie sheet and freeze 3 hours or overnight until very firm.

2. Melt the chocolate with the vegetable shortening, stirring frequently, until smooth. Pour into a tall mug or paper cup or other narrow container. Leave to cool 10–15 minutes, until thickened slightly.

3. Spread peanuts onto a small flat plate or sheet of foil. Hold the banana by the stick and dip into the melted chocolate, tilting the mug or cup and twisting until completely coated in chocolate. Quickly pull out banana and hold upright, then immediately roll in chopped nuts just until lightly coated.

4. Place on waxed paper-lined cookie sheet and freeze until firm. Continue coating each pop and place each on the prepared cookie sheet as soon as they are coated. Freeze at least 1 hour until chocolate is hardened. (Store pops covered in the freezer one to two weeks.)

TIP: Do not use metal sticks or small pointed wooden skewers as they could be harmful or cause injury to small children.

Rum-Raisin Surprise Bombe

10 SERVINGS

A rich frozen dessert, make this for a special occasion.

DOUBLE CHOCOLATE RUM-RAISIN ICE CREAM
1⁄2 cup raisins
1⁄4 cup plus 1 Tbsp light rum
5 oz good-quality white chocolate, chopped
1 oz (1 square) unsweetened chocolate, chopped
1 1⁄3 cups milk
3 egg yolks
2 Tbsp sugar
1⁄4 cup honey
1 cup heavy cream

WHITE CHOCOLATE MOUSSE
1⁄2 cup golden raisins
1⁄4 cup plus 1 Tbsp light rum
1 cup heavy cream
5 oz fine quality white chocolate, chopped
2 egg whites
1⁄4 tsp cream of tartar
1⁄4 cup superfine sugar

WHITE CHOCOLATE-RUM SAUCE
6 oz fine quality white chocolate
2⁄3 cup heavy cream
1⁄2 tsp ground cinnamon
1 Tbsp unsalted butter, softened
2 to 4 Tbsp dark or light rum

1. Prepare the ice cream: Soak the raisins in 1⁄4 cup rum for 2 hours.

2. Heat the white chocolate and unsweetened chocolate with 1⁄3 cup milk until melted.

3. Bring the remaining milk to a boil. With an electric mixer, beat the egg yolks with the sugar and honey until thickened. Whisk the hot milk into the yolk mixture and return to the heat. Cook until thickened. (Do not boil or mixture will curdle.) Stir into the melted chocolate mixture.

4. Strain the chocolate custard into the heavy cream and stir in the remaining rum. Chill, then transfer to an ice-cream maker and freeze as manufacturer directs. Spoon into a freezerproof container and stir in the rum-soaked raisins. Freeze until firm, but still spreadable; about 1 hour.

5. Chill a 1½ quart ice-cream bombe mold or freezerproof glass mixing bowl. Soften the ice cream slightly. Spread on base and up side of the chilled mold. Return to the freezer.

6. Prepare the mousse: Soak the golden raisins in ¼ cup rum for 2 hours. Bring ¼ cup cream to a boil. Stir in the white chocolate. Stir in the remaining rum and the rum-soaked raisins. Cool.

7. With an electric mixer, beat the egg whites until frothy. Add the cream of tartar and continue beating until stiff peaks form. Add the sugar a tablespoon at a time, beating well after each addition, until stiff and glossy. Fold into the white chocolate mixture.

8. Beat the remaining cream until soft peaks form. Fold into the mousse mixture. Spoon the white chocolate mousse into the center of the mold. Cover tightly and freeze overnight.

9. Prepare the sauce: Process the white chocolate in a food processor to fine crumbs. Bring the cream and cinnamon to a boil and with the machine running, pour in the hot cream. Strain into a bowl and stir in the butter and rum. Cool.

10. To serve: Unmold bombe and pipe a border of cream around the bottom edge and top. Soften in the refrigerator before serving with the sauce.

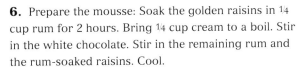

Frozen Chocolate-Coconut and Macadamia Terrine

8-10 SERVINGS

MOUSSE
8 oz fine quality white chocolate, chopped
2$\frac{1}{2}$ cups heavy cream
$\frac{1}{2}$ cup milk
10 egg yolks
2 Tbsp sugar
$\frac{1}{2}$ cup shredded coconut
$\frac{1}{2}$ cup canned sweetened coconut cream
2 Tbsp dark or light rum or 2 tsp rum extract
1$\frac{1}{4}$ cups unsalted macadamia nuts

DARK CHOCOLATE GLAZE
8 oz fine quality bittersweet or semisweet chocolate, chopped
6 Tbsp ($\frac{3}{4}$ stick) unsalted butter
1$\frac{1}{2}$ Tbsp light corn syrup
$\frac{3}{4}$ cup heavy cream

1. Line the bottom and sides of a 10 x 4-inch loaf pan or terrine with plastic wrap, smoothing out as many wrinkles as possible. Heat the white chocolate and $\frac{1}{4}$ cup cream until melted.

2. Bring 1 cup cream and the milk to a boil. With an electric mixer, beat the egg yolks with the sugar until thickened. Whisk the hot cream-milk mixture into the yolks and return to the heat. Cook until thickened. (Do not boil or the mixture will curdle.) Remove from heat and stir in the melted white chocolate mixture, shredded coconut, coconut cream, and rum. Cool in the refrigerator.

3. Beat the remaining cream until stiff peaks just begin to form. Fold into the mixture.

4. Spoon half the mousse mixture into the terrine. Cover and freeze until firm. Refrigerate the remaining mousse mixture.

5. When the mixture in the terrine is firm, sprinkle over the nuts. Spoon in the remaining mousse and freeze overnight.

6. Heat the glaze ingredients until melted. Invert the mousse onto a wire rack and lift off terrine. Pour the glaze over the top. Freeze 3–4 hours until set.

Frozen Raspberry Mousse-Ring

8 SERVINGS

My friend Carole gave me this recipe. It is a frozen mousse with a vibrant color and a creamy texture achieved by using a cooked meringue instead of a gelatin base.

1 lb (about 3$\frac{1}{2}$ cups) raspberries, plus extra for serving
$\frac{3}{4}$ cup superfine sugar
2 to 3 tsp lemon juice
2 egg whites
$\frac{1}{4}$ tsp cream of tartar
2 Tbsp raspberry-flavored liqueur
1 cup heavy cream

Fresh mint sprigs for decoration (optional)

1. Purée the raspberries in a food processor. Press through a nonmetallic sieve into a bowl. Pour about one third of the purée into a small bowl and stir in about $\frac{1}{4}$ cup sugar and a tablespoon of lemon juice. Add a little more sugar or lemon juice if necessary. Cover and refrigerate. Set aside remaining purée.

2. Put the egg whites, cream of tartar, 2 tablespoons lemon juice, and remaining ½ cup sugar in a large heatproof bowl and set over a saucepan of just simmering water. With an electric mixer, beat until the beaters leave a trail on the bottom of the bowl. Increase the speed to high, and continue beating until the whites are stiff and glossy, 7 minutes. Remove the bowl from heat and continue beating until mixture cools, about 3 minutes. Stir the raspberry-flavored liqueur into the remaining raspberry purée and fold into the meringue mixture.

3. Beat the cream until soft peaks form. Fold gently into the raspberry meringue mixture. Rinse a 6-cup ring mold and drain but do not dry. Spoon the mousse mixture into the mold. Freeze, covered, 4–6 hours or overnight.

4. To unmold, uncover the mold and run a sharp knife around the top edge. Dip into warm water for about 5 seconds and dry the base. Invert a serving plate over the mold then, holding the plate and mold together tightly, invert both together, giving a firm shake to release the mousse. Carefully remove the mold. To serve, fill the center of the mousse with raspberries and decorate with mint sprigs, if you like. Serve with the raspberry purée.

Pineapple-Pecan Ice Cream
with Pecan Butterscotch Sauce

6-8 SERVINGS

This is a delicious combination of flavors, which make an unusual summertime dessert.

ICE CREAM
1½ cups chopped fresh pineapple
¾ cup sugar
1 large egg
3 large egg yolks
1 Tbsp cornstarch
1½ cups milk
1 tsp vanilla
2 Tbsp dark rum (optional)
1½ cups heavy cream
1 cup broken pecan pieces, lightly toasted

PECAN BUTTERSCOTCH SAUCE
⅔ cup light corn syrup
1 cup light brown sugar, packed, plus 2 Tbsp
4 Tbsp butter (½ stick) cut into pieces
⅔ cup heavy cream

1. Prepare the ice cream: Simmer the pineapple and ¼ cup sugar, stirring occasionally until sugar dissolves, about 5 minutes. Turn into a nonmetallic strainer set over a bowl and allow to drain (reserve syrup for another use).

2. With a wire whisk, beat the egg and egg yolks with the remaining sugar until lightened in color and thickened, 3 minutes. Whisk in the cornstarch.

3. Bring the milk to a boil and pour over the egg mixture, beating constantly. Return mixture to the saucepan and cook, whisking, until mixture comes back to a boil. Boil 1 minute, whisking, then strain into a large bowl. Cool, then stir in the vanilla and pineapple mixture and refrigerate 1 hour.

4. Stir in the cream and transfer to an ice-cream maker. Freeze as manufacturer directs. Spoon into a container and stir in the toasted pecans to distribute them evenly, then freeze 2–3 hours or overnight.

5. Prepare the sauce: Bring the corn syrup, brown sugar, and butter to a boil until sugar has dissolved. Stir in the pecans and boil 2 minutes, remove from heat. Cool then stir in cream. Soften the ice cream slightly. Scoop into bowls and top with the sauce.

CHAPTER FIVE

CUSTARDS, MOUSSES, and SOUFFLES

Bittersweet Chocolate Mousse

6 SERVINGS

One of the world's favorite desserts—Try rum or orange-flavored liqueur for a change.

8 oz good-quality bittersweet chocolate, chopped
4 Tbsp water
2 Tbsp unsalted butter, softened
2 Tbsp cognac
3 large eggs, separated
1/4 tsp cream of tartar
2 to 3 Tbsp superfine sugar
1/2 cup heavy cream

1. Put the chocolate and water into a medium saucepan and melt over low heat until smooth, stirring frequently. Remove from heat and beat in the butter and cognac. Beat the egg yolks lightly then beat into the chocolate mixture; the chocolate will thicken. Set aside.

2. Beat the egg whites until frothy. Add the cream of tartar and continue to beat until soft peaks form. Beat in the sugar a tablespoon at a time, beating well after each addition until stiff and glossy. Beat a large spoonful of whites into the chocolate mixture to lighten it and reserve the remaining whites.

3. Beat the cream until soft peaks form. Reserve half the cream for decoration. Spoon half the cream over the chocolate mixture and fold into with remaining whites. Spoon into a glass serving bowl or into individual dessert dishes. Refrigerate overnight.

4. Spoon the remaining cream into a decorating bag fitted with a medium star nozzle and refrigerate. When the mousse is set, decorate with a rosette or scroll in the center of the bowl or on each individual dessert. Serve.

Strawberry-Mint Fools

4 SERVINGS

A fool is an old-fashioned dessert made from a fresh fruit purée swirled into whipped cream. It makes a quick and simple, but delicious, dessert. Look for ripe, full-flavored berries.

1 lb fresh ripe strawberries, hulled and quartered
3 to 4 Tbsp sugar
1 Tbsp fresh shredded mint
1/2 cup sour cream or plain yogurt
1/2 cup heavy cream

Fresh mint sprigs for decoration (optional)

1. Put the strawberries in a medium bowl and sprinkle with the sugar and the mint; the amount of sugar depends on the sweetness of the strawberries. Using a fork or potato masher, lightly crush the berries until the juices begin to run. Allow the mixture to stand about 20 minutes, stirring occasionally until all the sugar dissolves.

2. Strain the juices into a small bowl and whisk in the sour cream. Beat the cream until soft peaks form. Fold in the sour cream mixture.

3. Spoon alternate layers of crushed strawberries and cream into individual glass dessert dishes, ending with a layer of strawberries. Using a spoon or knife, gently swirl the layers in each dish, but do not mix well. Decorate with a mint sprig if you like.

_____

TIP: *Do not assemble too far in advance, or the cream and strawberries may become too liquid.*

Individual Sticky Toffee "Pudding" Cakes

4 SERVINGS

This typical British "pudding" or dessert is like a tiny moist sponge cake with a caramel-toffee sauce—cooked all in one.

CUSTARD SAUCE
(crème anglaise p.45)

CARAMEL-TOFFEE SAUCE
Melted butter for greasing
5 Tbsp sugar
2 Tbsp water
4 Tbsp heavy cream, heated

PUDDING CAKE
1/2 cup unsalted butter, softened
1/2 cup light brown sugar, packed
4 eggs, separated
1 cup self-rising flour or 1 cup all-purpose flour plus
1 tsp baking powder, sifted
1/4 cup chopped dates
Butter for greasing

1. Prepare the crème anglaise (p.45), but deleting the lemon zest and using the bean and tiny seeds of one vanilla bean. Stir in 1 tablespoon cornstarch into the beaten egg yolks and the sugar before whisking in the milk.

2. Prepare the caramel-toffee sauce: Butter four 1 1⁄4-cup custard cups or ramekins. Put the sugar in a saucepan and drizzle over the water to moisten. Cook over low heat until sugar dissolves. Boil until a golden caramel forms. Remove from heat and, standing well back, add the warm cream. Return to a heat and stir until melted and smooth.

3. Prepare the pudding cake: Preheat oven to 350°F. Beat the butter and sugar until fluffy and lightened in color, 2 minutes. Beat in the egg yolks one at a time,

beating well after each addition. Fold all but 2 to 3 tablespoons of the flour mixture into the butter-egg yolk mixture.

4. Beat the egg whites until soft peaks form. Stir a spoonful of whites into the mixture to lighten it, then fold in the remaining whites. Toss the dates in the reserved 2 to 3 tablespoons of the flour mixture and sprinkle over the batter, then gently fold in. Divide equally between the custard cups.

5. Cover each cup with greased baking parchment. Secure cup then cover with foil. Put cups in a larger roasting pan and pour in enough boiling water to come halfway up sides. Bake 40 minutes. Unmold and spoon over sauce. Serve with the custard.

Iced Lemon Soufflé with Caramel Syrup

6–8 SERVINGS

CARAMEL SYRUP
1 1⁄2 cups sugar
1⁄4 cup cold water
3⁄4 cup hot water

LEMON SOUFFLE
1⁄2 cup plus 2 Tbsp water
Grated zest and juice of 2 lemons
1 1⁄4 cups sugar
4 eggs, separated
2 Tbsp cold water
1 Tbsp (1 package) unflavored gelatin
1⁄4 tsp cream of tartar
1 1⁄4 cups heavy cream

1⁄2 cup heavy cream, whipped

1. Prepare the caramel syrup: Put the sugar in a saucepan and drizzle over the cold water to moisten. Heat until the sugar dissolves. Boil until syrup turns a deep caramel color, 10 minutes, without stirring. Remove from heat and, standing well back, add the hot water to the caramel; take care—the mixture will splatter. Return to the heat and stir until melted and smooth. Pour into a bowl and refrigerate.

2. Cut a piece of foil or waxed paper long enough to encircle a soufflé dish allowing a 2-inch overlap. Fold in half lengthwise and wrap around the dish so the collar extends about three inches above the top. Secure with string. Lightly oil the inside of the collar.

3. Prepare the lemon soufflé: Put the 1/2 cup water, lemon zest and juice, and sugar in a medium saucepan and boil for 5 minutes.

4. Process the egg yolks in a food processor for 30 seconds. With the machine running, slowly pour the boiling syrup onto the yolks and process 1 minute until creamy and pale.

5. Put 2 tablespoons of water in a small bowl and sprinkle over the gelatin. Allow to stand 2–3 minutes, then put into a small bowl and set over a saucepan of simmering water, stirring to dissolve. Add the gelatin to the egg mixture and process 5 seconds until blended. Pour into a large mixing bowl and refrigerate until mixture begins to set.

6. Beat the whites until frothy. Add the cream of tartar and beat on high speed until soft peaks form. Beat the cream until soft peaks form. Fold the cream into the chilled, setting-yolk mixture, then fold in the whites. Pour the mixture into the prepared dish. Refrigerate overnight.

7. Remove the string and peel the paper from the soufflé. Pipe rosettes or scrolls of whipped cream decoratively around the top edge. Serve immediately with the chilled caramel syrup.

Crème Brûlée
with Wild Strawberries

6 SERVINGS

Crème brûlée is an international favorite. The addition of wild strawberries makes it even more special. Try other berries and fruits if you like.

2 Tbsp unsalted butter, softened
4 Tbsp good quality strawberry jam
36 wild strawberries
4 cups heavy cream
1 vanilla bean, split lengthwise
6 egg yolks
1/2 cup superfine sugar
2 Tbsp orange-flavored liqueur or brandy
1/3 cup light brown sugar

1. Lightly butter six 1/2-cup ramekins. Stir the strawberry jam to loosen it, then divide it equally between the ramekins, spreading it even only on the bottoms. Put six wild strawberries in each ramekin and set them in a large roasting pan or ovenproof dish; set aside.

2. Preheat oven to 300°F. Put the cream in a medium saucepan. With a small sharp knife, scrape the tiny black seeds from the vanilla bean and add to the cream. Bring to a boil over medium-high heat, stirring frequently. Remove from heat, cover, and allow to stand for about 15 minutes.

3. Beat the egg yolks and sugar in a large bowl until foamy and lightened in color, 2–3 minutes. Bring the cream back to a boil and whisk into the egg yolk mixture until well-blended. Strain into a large measuring cup or pitcher, then divide the mixture equally among the prepared ramekins.

4. Pour enough boiling water into the roasting pan to come halfway up the sides of the ramekins. Cover the pan with foil and bake 25 minutes until the custards are just set (the centers should still be soft—do not overcook). Remove to a wire rack to cool completely then refrigerate overnight.

5. Preheat the broiler. Sprinkle an even layer of brown sugar over the surface of each custard and set them on a cookie sheet. Broil 30–60 seconds until the sugar melts and caramelizes, rotating the cookie sheet for even melting. (Do not allow the sugar to burn or the custard will curdle.) Refrigerate the crème brûlée immediately to stop cooking and allow the caramel to harden. Chill before serving.

Crème Caramel

6 SERVINGS

This is one of my all-time favorite recipes—the silky custard and slightly bitter caramel combine to make a classic dessert.

2 cups sugar
1/4 cup water
2 1/4 cups milk
3/4 cup heavy cream
1 vanilla bean, split lengthwise
4 large eggs
4 large yolks

1. Put one cup of the sugar in a heavy-based medium saucepan and drizzle over the water to moisten it. Set over medium-low heat until the sugar dissolves. Boil, without stirring, until the syrup turns a deep caramel; this will take about 6 minutes.

2. Immediately pour the hot caramel into a 6-cup soufflé dish or other heatproof mold and carefully swirl the dish to coat the bottom and sides evenly. Set aside to cool.

3. Preheat oven to 325°F. Put the milk and cream into a medium saucepan. With a small sharp knife, scrape the tiny black seeds from the vanilla bean and add to the milk and cream. Bring to a boil.

4. Whisk the eggs and egg yolks with the remaining sugar until foamy and lightened in color. Pour the boiling milk-mixture onto the egg mixture, whisking constantly. Carefully strain the custard into the caramel-lined dish and cover with foil.

5. Fold a dish towel and use to form a base in a large roasting pan or dish. Set the soufflé dish or mold onto the towel and pour in enough boiling water to come halfway up the side. Bake 40–45 minutes or until just set. Carefully remove to a wire rack to cool about 30 minutes. Refrigerate 6–8 hours or overnight.

6. To unmold, carefully run a sharp knife around the edge of the dish to loosen the custard. Cover the dish with a serving plate and, holding them tightly, invert the dish and plate together. Gently lift one side of the soufflé dish or mold, allowing the caramel to run over the side, then lift off the dish. Cut in wedges and serve with a little caramel.

Floating Island
with Blackcurrant Coulis

6 SERVINGS

Floating island gets its name from the molded meringue sitting in a pool of custard sauce or crème anglaise. This version uses a blackcurrant coulis to glaze the meringue island instead of the traditional caramel.
Use any other favorite berry if blackcurrants are unavailable.

BLACKCURRANT COULIS
1 lb fresh blackcurrants, stalks removed, rinsed and drained, or frozen blackcurrants (thawed)
1/4 cup water
1/4 cup sugar
2 Tbsp lemon juice

MERINGUE
4 egg whites
1/4 tsp cream of tartar
1/2 cup superfine sugar
1 tsp vanilla extract
Crème Anglaise (p.45)

Chopped filberts or pistachios for decoration

1. Process the blackcurrants, water, sugar, and lemon juice in a food processor. Press through a non-metallic strainer into a bowl. Refrigerate.

2. Prepare the crème anglaise as for lemon crème anglaise (p.45), but deleting the lemon zest and adding one vanilla bean with its seeds to the milk. Alternatively, flavor with 2 teaspoons vanilla extract.

3. Prepare the meringue. Preheat oven to 350°F. Lightly butter a 4- or 5-cup charlotte mold or soufflé dish. Beat the egg whites until frothy. Add the cream of tartar and continue beating until stiff peaks form. Add the sugar 2 tablespoons at a time, beating well after each addition, folding in the last 2 tablespoons of sugar with the vanilla. Spoon into the mold.

4. Set the mold or dish into a deep roasting pan and pour in enough boiling water to come at least 1-inch up the sides. Bake about 25 minutes until the top is golden and springy to the touch. Cool and then refrigerate overnight.

5. Unmold onto a large shallow serving dish. Ladle the crème anglaise around the meringue island and spoon the blackcurrant coulis over the top of the meringue. Sprinkle the top with the filberts or pistachios and serve.

Creamy Rice Pudding
with Tropical Fruits

8–10 SERVINGS

3½ cups milk
1 cup heavy cream
⅔ cup short-grain rice
1 vanilla bean, split lengthwise
2 to 4 Tbsp sugar
2 Tbsp golden raisins
2 eggs
½ tsp ground cinnamon
¼ tsp allspice

3 cups chopped chopped fruits, such as mango, kiwi, papaya, melon, grapes, peeled lychees, and strawberries
3 Tbsp brown sugar for sprinkling

Fresh mint sprigs for decoration

1. Put the milk, cream, rice, split vanilla bean, sugar, and golden raisins into a large heavy-based saucepan or casserole. Bring to a boil over medium heat, then reduce the heat to low and simmer about 20 minutes, stirring frequently.

2. Whisk the eggs in a small bowl and pour in a little of the milky rice mixture, beating well. Slowly pour the egg mixture back into the rice mixture, stirring constantly. Cook over low heat until the mixture thickens, about 1 minute. (Do not boil or the eggs will curdle.) Remove from heat and stir in the cinnamon and allspice and pour into a large bowl. Cool slightly, stirring occasionally to prevent a skin from forming.

3. Spoon the warm pudding into a shallow serving bowl and arrange the fruit over the top. Sprinkle the brown sugar over the fruit, decorate with the fresh mint sprigs and serve while still warm. Alternatively, refrigerate the pudding and serve cold with the fruit.

Cherry-Cheese Blintzes
with Cherry Cognac Sauce

ABOUT 12 BLINTZES

Blintzes are a Jewish-American treat made by filling thin crêpes with a sweetened soft-cheese mixture, then folding and frying them. They are delicious with this cherry cognac sauce.

FOR THE CREPES
⅔ cup all-purpose flour, sifted
½ tsp salt
2 Tbsp superfine sugar
2 eggs, lightly beaten
1 cup milk
¼ cup water
2 Tbsp cognac (optional)
2 Tbsp unsalted butter, melted, plus extra for frying

DRIED CHERRY-CHEESE FILLING
¼ cup dried sour cherries
¼ cup hot water
1 cup creamed cottage cheese or ricotta cheese
1 (3-oz) package cream cheese, softened
3 to 4 Tbsp sugar
½ tsp vanilla extract

CHERRY COGNAC SAUCE
1 lb sweet cherries, pitted
½ cup cognac
½ cup sugar
2 tsp cornstarch dissolved in 1½ Tbsp cold water

2 to 4 Tbsp butter for frying

1. Prepare the crêpes: Sift the flour, salt, and sugar into a bowl and make a well in the center. Pour in the beaten egg and whisk in the eggs and then the milk and water until a smooth batter forms. Stir in the cognac, if using, and strain into a large measuring cup. Allow to stand about 30 minutes.

2. Heat a small nonstick crêpe pan. Stir the melted butter into the crêpe batter and brush the hot pan with a little of the extra melted butter. Pour in 2–3 tablespoons of batter and rotate the pan covering the bottom with a thin layer of batter. Cook until the top is set and the bottom is golden brown, about 1 minute. Turn and cook the other side for 30 seconds until set. Slide onto a plate. Cook the remaining crêpes in the same way.

3. Prepare the cheese mixture: Soak the dried cherries in the hot water for about 20 minutes. In a large bowl beat the cottage cheese or ricotta cheese, cream cheese, sugar, and vanilla until smooth; stir in the dried cherries.

4. Spread a little of the cheese mixture along the center of each crêpe and roll up.

5. Prepare the sauce: Bring the cherries, cognac, and sugar to a boil in a saucepan. Stir the cornstarch mixture, then stir into the cherry liquid and boil until thick, about 1 minute.

6. Heat 2 to 3 tablespoons butter in a large skillet. Add the blintzes in batches if necessary, and cook until golden on both sides, about 3 minutes. Serve immediately with the hot sauce.

Chocolate Tiramisù

10–12 SERVINGS

Tiramisù translates as "pick-me-up." This classic Italian dessert will do more than pick you up, it will transport you to heaven.

1 (17½-oz) container mascarpone* cheese, at room temperature
½ cup confectioners' sugar, sifted
1½ cups freshly brewed espresso or strong coffee, chilled
2½ cups heavy cream
6 oz good-quality bittersweet or semisweet chocolate, melted and cooled
6 Tbsp coffee-flavored liqueur
2 oz bittersweet or semisweet chocolate, grated
2 Tbsp chocolate-flavored liqueur
1 (7-oz) package savoiardi** cookies (imported Italian ladyfingers)
Cocoa powder for dusting, sifted

1. Put the mascarpone and sugar in a large bowl and, with an electric mixer, beat until smooth and creamy, about 1 minute. Gradually beat in about ¼ cup espresso or strong coffee; do not overbeat.

2. Beat the cream until soft peaks form. Gently fold the cream into the mascarpone mixture, then spoon half the mixture back into the cream bowl. Fold the melted chocolate and 2 tablespoons of the coffee-flavored liqueur into half the mascarpone-cream mixture and set aside. Fold the grated chocolate and the chocolate-flavored liqueur into the remaining mascarpone cream mixture; set aside.

3. Put half the remaining espresso or strong coffee and 2 tablespoons coffee-flavored liqueur in a shallow dish. Dip one side of a savoiardi cookie into the coffee mixture and plate it dry-side down in a 13 x 9-inch baking dish. Continue with half the cookies to form a lightly packed layer. Drizzle over any remaining espresso or coffee mixture. Spoon the chocolate-mascarpone mixture over the cookie layer in the dish, smoothing the surface evenly.

4. Pour the remaining coffee and liqueur into the dish. Dip the remaining cookies into the espresso mixture, layering them over the chocolate mascarpone mixture. Drizzle over any remaining espresso or coffee mixture. Spoon the remaining grated chocolate-mascarpone mixture over the second layer of cookies and smooth the top, leaving no spaces between the filling and sides of the dish. Cover the dish with plastic wrap and refrigerate overnight. To serve, dust with a thick layer of cocoa.

*Mascarpone is a smooth, sweet Italian cream cheese, available in large supermarkets and gourmet shops.

**Savoiardi cookies are imported Italian/French ladyfingers, with a crisp finish.

Chocolate Pavlova
with Exotic Fruits and White Chocolate Cream

6–8 SERVINGS

Both Australia and New Zealand claim to have invented this delicate meringue-based dessert to honor the famous ballerina, Anna Pavlova. This is a chocolate version.

MERINGUE
4 egg whites, at room temperature
¼ tsp cream of tartar
1 cup superfine sugar
3 Tbsp unsweetened cocoa powder, sifted
1 tsp cornstarch
1 tsp cider vinegar

WHITE CHOCOLATE CREAM
4 oz good-quality white chocolate, chopped
1/2 cup light cream or half-and-half
1 Tbsp unsalted butter
1 tsp vanilla extract
1 cup heavy cream
4 cups sliced mixed exotic fruits such as kiwi, mango,
papaya or 4 cups mixed strawberries, raspberries,
and blueberries

Fresh mint sprigs for decoration

1. Preheat oven to 325°F. Place a sheet of non-stick baking parchment on a large baking sheet and, using a plate as a guide, draw an 8-inch circle.

2. With an electric mixer, beat the egg whites until frothy. Add the cream of tartar and continue beating until stiff peaks form. Sprinkle in the sugar, 2 tablespoons at a time, making sure each addition is well-blended before adding the next, until whites are stiff and glossy. Fold in the sifted cocoa and cornstarch mixture then fold in the vinegar.

3. Spoon the meringue mixture onto the center of the circle marked on the paper. Using the back of a metal spoon spread evenly, building up the sides higher than the center. Bake in the center of the oven until set, 45–50 minutes. Turn off the oven and leave to stand in the oven 45 minutes longer; the meringue may crack or sink, but it does not matter. Cool the meringue completely and carefully transfer to a serving plate.

4. Heat the white chocolate and single cream or half-and-half until smooth. Beat in the butter and vanilla and cool.

5. Beat the cream until soft peaks form. Stir half the cream into the chocolate mixture, then fold in the remaining cream and spoon into the center of the meringue. Arrange the fruits over the white chocolate cream and decorate with the mint.

Panna Cotta
with Fresh Apricot Compote

6 SERVINGS

APRICOT COMPOTE

1 lb fresh apricots
1/4 tsp ground cinnamon
1/4 cup sugar
1 1/2 cups water
1/2 tsp almond extract

PANNA COTTA

3 cups heavy cream
1 vanilla bean
3 to 4 tsp sugar
1 cup milk
1 1/2 packages unflavored gelatin (about 1 1/2 Tbsp)

Slivered toasted almonds for decoration

1. Plunge the apricots into boiling water for 20 seconds. With a small sharp knife, peel off the skins.

2. Pit the apricots and chop. Put in a saucepan with the cinnamon and sugar. Add the water, enough to cover the fruit, and bring to a boil. Simmer 10 minutes until fruit is tender and syrup thickened. Remove from heat, stir in almond extract and cool.

3. Pour the cream into a saucepan. Split the vanilla bean lengthwise and scrape the black seeds into the cream; add the vanilla bean then stir in the sugar. Bring to a boil. Cool and remove the vanilla bean.

4. Pour the milk into a small saucepan and sprinkle over the gelatin. Allow to stand until spongy and transparent. Set the pan over low heat and heat, stirring to dissolve the gelatin. Stir the gelatin-milk mixture into the cream mixture and leave to cool, stirring occasionally. Divide between six 3/4-cup ramekins and refrigerate overnight.

5. Unmold and sprinkle the panna cotta with almonds. Spoon a little compote onto each plate.

Pots de Crème

8 SERVINGS

2 cups milk
2 Tbsp instant coffee powder, dissolved in
2 Tbsp hot water
1/2 cup sugar
8 oz fine-quality bittersweet chocolate, chopped
2 Tbsp coffee-flavored liqueur or brandy
1 Tbsp vanilla extract
7 egg yolks
Whipped cream and finely chopped pistachios for decoration

1. Preheat oven to 300°F. Bring the milk, dissolved instant coffee, and sugar to a boil. Add the chocolate all at once; remove from heat and stir until melted and smooth. Stir in the coffee-flavored liqueur and the vanilla extract.

2. Beat the egg yolks until blended but not too frothy. Slowly beat the chocolate mixture into the yolks. Strain into a large measuring cup or pitcher.

3. Arrange eight 1/2-cup pot de crème cups, custard cups or ramekins in a shallow roasting pan. Divide the mixture between the cups. Pour enough hot water into the pan to come about halfway up the side of the cups. Cover the pan with foil.

4. Bake about 30 minutes until the custard is just set. Alternatively, insert a knife-blade into the side of one cup, it should come out clean. Remove the pan from the oven and remove the cups from the pan to a heatproof surface to cool completely.

5. Place the cups on a cookie sheet and cover with plastic wrap. Refrigerate 3–4 hours or overnight. To serve, decorate the top of each pot de crème with a rosette of whipped cream and a sprinkle of chopped pistachios.

Bittersweet Chocolate Soufflés
with White Chocolate Orange Sauce

6 SERVINGS

These delicious soufflés make a spectacular presentation for a special dinner party.

WHITE CHOCOLATE ORANGE SAUCE
3 oz fine quality white chocolate, chopped
1/3 cup heavy cream
2 Tbsp orange-flavored liqueur
2 Tbsp freshly squeezed orange juice, strained

Softened butter for coating
Granulated sugar for sprinkling
4 oz bittersweet or semisweet chocolate, chopped
1/4 cup (1/2 stick) unsalted butter
4 eggs, separated
2 Tbsp orange-flavored liqueur
1/4 tsp cream of tartar
2 Tbsp superfine sugar
Confectioners' sugar for dusting, sifted

1. Prepare the sauce: Melt the white chocolate with the cream. Stir in the orange-flavored liqueur and juice. Strain into a serving bowl and set aside.

2. Preheat oven to 425°F. Butter six 2/3-cup ramekins and chill for 5 minutes. Butter again and sprinkle with a tablespoon of sugar. Arrange on a cookie sheet for easier handling.

3. Heat the chocolate and butter until melted. Remove from heat and beat in the egg yolks one at a time, beating well after each addition. Beat in the orange-flavored liqueur.

4. Beat the whites until frothy. Add the cream of tartar and beat until stiff peaks form. Sprinkle over the superfine sugar and beat 1 minute.

5. Stir one quarter of the beaten whites into the chocolate mixture then fold the mixture into the remaining whites. Do not overwork. Divide among the chilled dishes. Bake 12 minutes until the tops are set and risen; the centers should remain slightly soft. Dust with confectioners' sugar and serve.

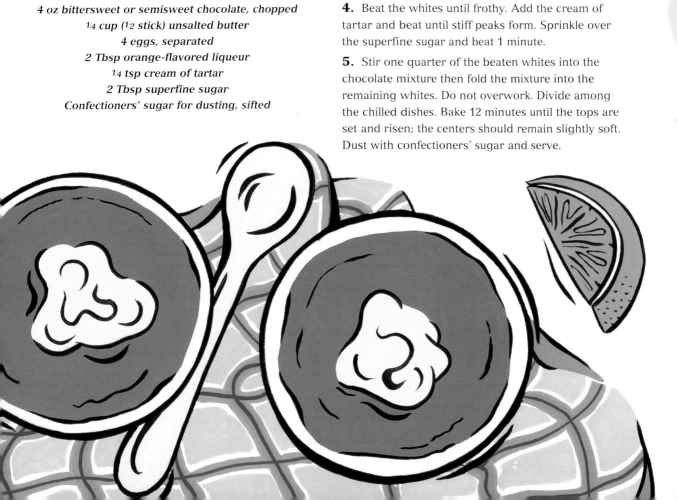

Crunchy Amaretto Soufflé

6 SERVINGS

Softened butter for greasing
Sugar for sprinkling

6 Amaretti cookies, lightly crushed
⅓ cup Amaretto liqueur
1 cup milk
4 eggs, separated
½ cup superfine sugar
2 Tbsp all-purpose flour, sifted
1 egg white
Confectioners' sugar for dusting, sifted

1. Preheat oven to 400°F. Generously butter the base and sides of a 5- to 6-cup soufflé dish. Refrigerate until set, butter again and sprinkle with sugar.

2. Put the crushed cookies in a small bowl and sprinkle with half the liqueur; set aside.

3. Bring the milk to a boil. Beat the eggs and half the sugar until foamy and lightened, 2 minutes. Stir in the flour until just blended. Whisk the hot milk into the egg mixture. Return to the saucepan and cook until thickened, stirring constantly; about 5 minutes. Remove from heat and whisk in remaining liqueur.

4. Beat all the egg whites until soft peaks form. Gradually beat in the remaining sugar and continue beating until stiff and glossy. Stir a spoonful of whites into the egg-yolk mixture to lighten it, the fold in the remaining whites until just blended (do not overmix).

5. Spoon half the mixture into the dish and cover with the Amaretti cookie-liqueur mixture. Spoon over the remaining soufflé mixture, smoothing the top. Tap the dish gently to release large air bubbles.

6. Bake 25 minutes until well risen and golden. It should wobble when dish is moved gently. Remove to a heatproof dish, dust with sugar, and serve.

Apricot-Glazed Panettone Bread Pudding

8–10 SERVINGS

2 Tbsp golden raisins
3 Tbsp unsalted butter, softened to room temperature
6 medium slices panettone
2 cups milk
2¼ cups heavy cream
1 vanilla bean, split in half lengthwise
6 large eggs
1¼ cups sugar

APRICOT GLAZE
⅓ cup apricot preserves

Confectioners' sugar for dusting, sifted

1. Soak the golden raisins in hot water. Brush a large oval baking dish with some of the butter. Butter the slices of panettone with remaining butter and arrange them in the bottom of the dish, cutting to fit. Drain the raisins and sprinkle over the panettone.

2. Preheat oven to 325°F. Pour the milk and cream into a saucepan. Scrape the seeds from the vanilla bean and add to milk and cream. Bring to a boil.

3. Whisk the eggs with the sugar until foamy and lightened in color. Pour the milk-cream mixture onto the egg mixture, whisking. Strain over the panettone.

4. Fold a dish towel and use to form a base in a large roasting pan or dish. Set the baking dish on the towel and pour in enough boiling water to come halfway up the sides of the baking dish. Bake about 50 minutes; the center should be wobbly. Cool slightly.

5. Heat the apricot preserves with 2 to 3 tablespoons of water until melted and smooth. Press through a sieve set over a small bowl. Brush the apricot glaze over the top. Allow to cool until pudding is just warm. Dust with confectioners' sugar before serving.

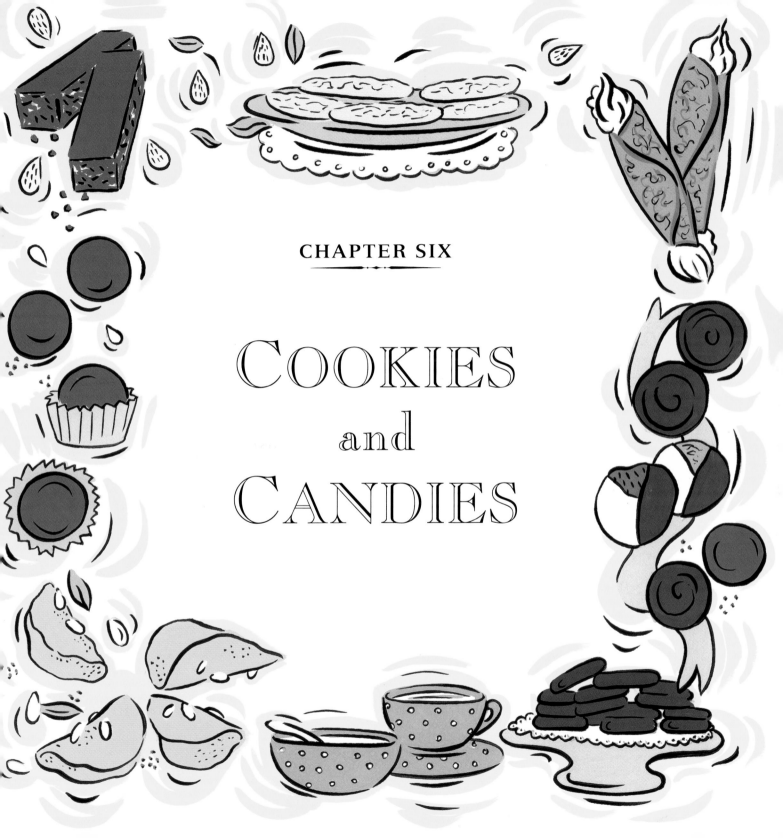

CHAPTER SIX

COOKIES
and
CANDIES

Chocolate Mint Crisps

MAKES ABOUT 24 MINTS

These easy-to-make after-dinner mints are perfect with a coffee. As an alternative, use orange extract instead of mint.

Vegetable oil for greasing
4 Tbsp sugar
¼ cup water
1 tsp mint extract
8 oz bittersweet or semisweet chocolate, chopped

1. Using a pastry brush, brush a cookie sheet with vegetable oil and set aside.

2. Put the sugar in a saucepan with the water and bring to a boil over medium heat, swirling pan until sugar dissolves. Boil rapidly until the sugar reaches 280°F on a candy thermometer. Remove from heat and swirl in the mint extract. Pour onto the greased cookie sheet and allow to cool completely. Do not touch, as sugar syrup is hot and can cause serious burns.

3. When cold and hard, lift off the cookie sheet and break into small pieces. Put the pieces into the bowl of a food processor fitted with a metal blade and process until fine crumbs form; do not overprocess.

4. Line two cookie sheets with nonstick baking parchment or foil. Put the chocolate in a small bowl and set over a saucepan of just simmering water. Stir frequently until melted and smooth. Remove from heat and stir in the ground sugar-mint mixture.

5. Using a teaspoon, drop small mounds of the mixture onto prepared cookie sheets. Using the back of a spoon, spread into 1½-inch circles. Cool, then refrigerate until set, at least 1 hour. Peel the chocolate mints off the paper and refrigerate in an airtight container with waxed paper between each layer.

TIP: If you do not have a candy thermometer, test the temperature of the boiling sugar by pouring a few drops of syrup into a small bowl of cold water; it should become brittle and snap easily within 1 minute. Do not touch the sugar until it cools in the water for a few seconds.

Chocolate Truffles

ABOUT 24 TRUFFLES

Most truffles are made from a ganache base—a mixture of chocolate and cream or butter with the addition of a flavoring such as cognac or another liqueur. Truffles can be rolled in cocoa or finely chopped nuts, or dipped in chocolate.

1 cup heavy cream
10 oz fine-quality bittersweet chocolate, chopped
2 Tbsp unsalted butter
2 Tbsp brandy or other favorite liqueur

Cocoa powder for dusting, sifted
1 lb bittersweet chocolate

1. Bring the cream to a boil. Remove from heat and add the chocolate all at once, stirring until melted and smooth. Beat in the butter until melted and stir in the liqueur. Strain into a bowl and cool to room temperature. Refrigerate until thickened and firm, about 1 hour.

2. Line a cookie sheet with foil or nonstick baking parchment. With a teaspoon, form mixture into small balls and place on the prepared cookie sheet.

3. If dusting with cocoa, sift about 1⁄2 cup cocoa powder into a small bowl. Drop each ball into the cocoa and toss with a fork to coat on all sides, then roll lightly between the palms of your hands, rounding the balls. (Dust your hands with cocoa to prevent the truffles from sticking.) Do not worry if the truffles are not perfectly round as an irregular shape is more authentic.

4. Shake cocoa-coated truffles in a dry strainer to remove any excess cocoa. Refrigerate covered in an airtight container for up to 2 weeks, or freeze for up to 2 months. Soften slightly at room temperature before serving.

5. If coating with melted chocolate, do not roll in cocoa, but freeze for 1 hour after forming into balls. Melt the bittersweet chocolate in a small bowl and, using a fork, dip balls into melted chocolate one at a time, tapping fork on side of bowl to shake off excess. Place on the prepared cookie sheet and refrigerate immediately to keep coating shiny. (If melted chocolate thickens, reheat gently to thin.)

Almond Tile Cookies

15 COOKIES

These popular French cookies—tuiles aux amandes—are so called because they resemble the curved roof tiles seen all over France. Although they are not difficult to make, they do require a little patience and practice in the beginning.

1⁄2 cup whole blanched almonds, lightly toasted
1⁄2 cup superfine sugar
3 Tbsp unsalted butter, softened
2 egg whites
1⁄2 tsp almond extract
1⁄4 cup cake flour, sifted
3⁄4 cup slivered almonds

1. Process the blanched almonds and 2 tablespoons of the sugar in a food processor until fine crumbs form. Pour into a small bowl and set aside.

2. Preheat oven to 400°F. Generously butter two or more cookie sheets. With an electric mixer, beat the butter until creamy, about 1 minute. Add the remaining sugar and beat until light and fluffy. Gradually beat in the egg whites and almond extract until well-blended. Re-sift the already sifted flour and fold into the butter mixture, then fold in the reserved almond-sugar mixture.

3. Begin by working in batches of four cookies on each sheet. Drop tablespoons of batter about 6 inches apart onto cookie sheet. With the back of a moistened spoon, spread each mound of batter into very thin 3-inch rounds. Each round should be transparent; it does not matter if you make a few holes, the batter will spread evenly and fill them in. Sprinkle tops with some slivered almonds.

4. Bake, one sheet at a time, for about 5 minutes. Remove cookie sheet to wire rack and, working quickly, use a thin-bladed metal spatula to loosen the edge of a hot cookie. Transfer to a rolling pin or glass tumbler and gently press sides down to shape each cookie. Repeat with the remaining cookie rounds.

5. If cookies become too firm to transfer, return the cookie sheet to the oven for 30 seconds to soften, then proceed as above. Continue baking and shaping with the remaining dough. When cool transfer immediately to airtight containers in single layers. These cookies are fragile.

TIP: If cookies become limp, reshape by placing cookies on an ungreased baking sheet and baking again at 100°F until completely flattened, 2–3 minutes. Reshape over rolling pin as instructed above.

Cream-Filled Brandy Snaps

ABOUT 2½ DOZEN

These lacy cognac-scented cookies are filled with a cognac-flavored whipped cream. Sometimes called "English Rolled Wafers," they make an elegant after-dinner treat.

BRANDY SNAPS
Butter for greasing
½ cup (1 stick) unsalted butter, cut into pieces
3 Tbsp corn syrup
¼ cup sugar
¼ cup light brown sugar, packed
1 tsp ground ginger
2 Tbsp cognac
½ cup all-purpose flour, sifted

COGNAC CREAM
1¼ cups heavy cream
1 Tbsp sugar
½ tsp vanilla extract
2 Tbsp cognac

1. Preheat oven to 350°F. Butter two or more baking sheets; or use nonstick baking sheets. Lightly oil the handles of two wooden spoons. Put the butter, corn syrup, sugars, and ginger in a saucepan and bring to a boil over medium heat, stirring until sugars dissolve. Remove from heat, stir in the cognac and the flour until well-blended and smooth. Place the saucepan in a shallow bowl of hot water (this will keep the batter from hardening).

2. Working in batches of four cookies on each baking sheet, drop tablespoons of batter about 6 inches apart on the sheets. Using the back of a moistened spoon, spread each mound into 3-inch rounds (the rounds will spread out even more). Bake until golden and bubbling, about 10 minutes, turning the baking sheet if the brandy snaps color unevenly.

3. Remove the baking sheet to a wire rack to cool, about 1 minute. Working quickly, use a thin-bladed metal spatula to loosen the edge of a hot brandy snap and lift it off. Roll each cookie around the oiled handle of a wooden spoon. Slide off the handle and transfer to a wire rack to cool completely.

4. Up to 2 hours before serving, with an electric mixer, beat the cream, sugar, vanilla, and brandy until stiff peaks form. Spoon cream into a decorating bag fitted with a medium star nozzle. Pipe cream into both ends of each cookie and place on a baking sheet. Refrigerate until ready to serve.

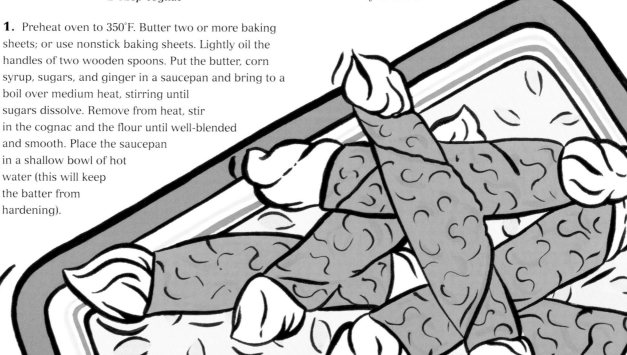

After-Dinner Chocolate Cream Liqueur

Surprise your guests with this homemade chocolate cream liqueur. For a real show stopper, serve with a chocolate truffle in the middle and a tiny spoon.

1 Tbsp instant espresso or coffee powder
1/4 cup unsweetened cocoa powder, sifted
1 cup milk
1 cup heavy cream
1 (14-oz) can sweetened condensed milk
1 egg yolk
1 cup Scotch whisky
1/3 cup light rum
1 Tbsp vanilla extract
1 Tbsp coconut extract

1. Stir together the espresso or coffee powder and cocoa powder in a large saucepan. Gradually whisk in the milk then the cream and sweetened condensed milk and bring to a boil over medium heat, stirring frequently until well-blended.

2. Beat the egg yolk in a small bowl until foamy. Pour half the hot-milk mixture over the yolk, whisking constantly, then stir the cream-egg mixture back into the saucepan. Cook over medium-low heat until the mixture thickens slightly and coats the back of a wooden spoon, about 3 minutes. Remove from heat and stir in the whisky, rum, and vanilla and coconut extracts. Strain into a bowl and cool, stirring constantly. Refrigerate until completely chilled, about 3–4 hours.

3. Transfer to a bottle or jar with a tight-fitting lid and store in the refrigerator for up to 1 week. Stir or shake well before serving.

Double Chocolate-Dipped Fruit

ABOUT 12 PIECES

About 12 pieces of fruit such as strawberries, cherries, Cape gooseberries, orange segments, kiwi fruit, pitted prunes, pitted dates, dried apricots, dried pears
6 oz good-quality white chocolate, chopped
3 oz good-quality bittersweet or semisweet chocolate, chopped

1. Clean and prepare the fruits. Wipe strawberries with a soft cloth or brush gently with a pastry brush; wash firm fruits like cherries or grapes, dry well and set on paper towels to absorb any remaining moisture. Peel or cut any other fruits being used and choose the plumpest dried fruits. Line a baking sheet with nonstick baking parchment or foil.

2. Put the white chocolate in a small heatproof bowl and set over a saucepan of hot water. Stir frequently until melted and smooth. Remove from heat and then cool slightly.

3. Holding fruits by the stem or end and at an angle, dip about two thirds of the fruit into the chocolate. Allow excess to drip off and place on the prepared baking sheet. Continue dipping all the fruits; if the chocolate becomes too thick, heat gently over the hot water to thin. Refrigerate until set, about 30 minutes.

4. Put the bittersweet chocolate into another small heatproof bowl and set over a saucepan of hot water. Stir frequently until melted and smooth. Remove from heat and cool slightly.

5. Lift the half-coated fruits from the baking sheet and, holding each piece by the stem or end, and at the opposite angle, dip bottom third of each piece into the chocolate, creating a chevron effect. Set on the lined cookie sheet and refrigerate until set. Soften slightly at room temperature before serving.

Index